15,105

HG
353
.B47
1973b

Beresiner
The story of
paper money

DATE DUE

JE 13 84			
OC 18 84			
NO 26 84			
JE 12 85			

Yasha Beresiner and Colin Narbeth

The Story of Paper Money

Arco Publishing Company, Inc. : New York

Published 1973 by Arco Publishing Company, Inc.
219 Park Avenue South, New York, N.Y. 10003
Second Printing 1975
Copyright © 1973 by Yasha Beresiner and C. C. Narbeth

Library of Congress Catalogue Card Number 72-92286

ISBN 0-668-02905-6

Printed in Great Britain

Contents

Introduction

The history of money reflects the history of civilisation. Today ninety per cent of the world's financial transactions are carried out with paper money, and we can learn a great deal from its use throughout history. The study of paper money issues has been neglected in the past, and it is particularly interesting now as new information is continually coming to light.

It is ironical that a numismatist can look at a coin thousands of years old and very often quickly date it, yet a notaphilist can sometimes have difficulty in dating a note which is less than fifty years old! Although the serious study of paper money is comparatively new its use is much older than most people realise—it was in the time of the Great Khan that China experienced its first paper inflation.

This book sets out to present a brief glimpse at some of the fascinating history that lies behind notes. The popularity of the hobby is such that banknotes are, like stamps, collected by subjects and themes as well as by countries. Many countries have been left out altogether because of lack of space, but we hope the reader will find our selection of more than passing interest.

Because the finest engravers were employed in the production of notes, a private collection can be a miniature art gallery in itself. It was not because the issuers particularly wanted fine art, but simply to make forgery more difficult. The result, however, is that the collector amasses some really beautiful designs.

At certain times, such as during World War II, emergency issues of paper money were made and are today the only tangible relics of specific occasions. Their value to history, therefore, is of great importance—notes that readily come to mind are siege notes of Mafeking and Khartoum, concentration camp notes and partisan issues.

The reader will find some illustrations are overprinted SPECIMEN. This is because it is not permitted to reproduce certain banknotes except in such manner and with permission from the authorities concerned.

1: Early Paper Money

CHINA

Paper was invented by the Chinese about AD 200 and it was China which produced the world's first paper money. Historical sources refer to a note issue in AD 650 though none of the notes exist. Several issues were made during the Sung dynasty: exchangeable money (*dijau-dze*) and citadel money (*quei-dze*); but these were not banknotes in the modern sense of the term.

The warrior Mongols under the famous Kublai Khan were the first to make large note issues. The Mongols did something which has become common practice throughout history. Unable to pay their soldiers, they simply used the printing press and issued military money. The soldiers had no option but to accept this money. Within ten years, however, the Mongols were obliged to relinquish their hold on China and leave. By 1358 their paper money had become worth-

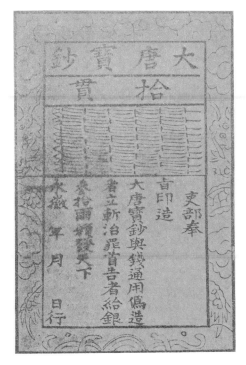

1 *The earliest known bank-note in the world. A ten-kwan note of the Tang dynasty, AD 650-6. This is a copy of the illustration in Ch'uan Pu T'ung Chih, an early Chinese historical work. The actual size of the note is $9 \times 5\frac{7}{8}$in*

9

2 Ming dynasty banknote c 1368 for 1000 cash

to light following the Boxer Rebellion in 1900 and was sold in America at that time for $3,600. When others appeared the price dropped considerably and they are now fetching between £300 and £400.

The Ming notes, mainly issued in 1368, lasted until about 1450 when banknotes were abolished in China. Notes other than the first issue of 1368 are recorded but not known to exist. The next paper money in China did not come until the Tai Ping Rebellion in the 1850s.

A full description of the early notes of China, identical to the Ming issues, is given to us by Marco Polo. A Venetian born in 1254, Marco Polo went with his father and uncle on a mission from the Pope to the court of Kublai Khan in Cathay in 1271. Later he went to Peking and so impressed the court that he was made a court official. His description of paper money was as follows:

All these pieces of paper are issued with as much solemnity and authority as if they were of pure gold or silver; and on every piece a variety of officials, whose duty it is, have to write their names, and put their seals. And when all is prepared duly, the chief officer deputed by the Khan smears the seal entrusted to him with vermilion, and impresses it on the paper, so that the form of the seal remains printed upon it on red; the money is then authentic. And the Khan causes every year to be made such a vast quantity of this money, which costs him nothing, that it must be equal in amount to all the treasure in the world.

When any of those pieces of paper are spoilt—not that they are so very flimsy either—the owners carry them to the mint, and by paying three per

less. The only known examples of this money are now in the Peking Museum.

The Ming dynasty which followed (1368-1644) started with an issue of notes almost identical to the Mongol notes— these are the earliest notes which it is possible for a collector to obtain as some twenty or thirty have come on the market since 1900. The first of these notes came

cent on the value can get new pieces in exchange.

Marco Polo concludes: 'Now you have heard the ways and means whereby the great Khan may have, and in fact has, more treasure than all the kings in the world.' Many students of history regard Marco Polo as given to 'racy descriptions' but in the case of paper money he is supported by a number of other contemporary writers: William de Rubruquis, Roger Bacon, Hayton, Pegollotti, Josafat Barbara, Ibn Batuta and Ahmed Shibab Eddi.

The Ming notes were printed from wooden blocks and issued as imperial banknotes by the Emperor T'Aitsu-Hung Wu-Ming, founder of the Ming dynasty. Coloured dark slate, they are in the denomination of one kwan or 'one string of cash.' The inscription, in Chinese characters, at the top of the note reads, 'Government of the Ming Empire' and the borders are attractively designed in arabesque style with dragons. In the centre are two panels.

The top panel reads 'One Kwan' and underneath are pictorial illustrations of ten hundreds of cash. On the side of the panel is a square seal which somewhat hopefully can be translated: 'Government Note of the Ming Empire circulating for Ever and Ever.'

That the Chinese feared forgery is evident from the lower panel which reads: 'The Imperial Board of Revenue, having memorialized the Throne, has received the Imperial sanction for the issue of Government notes of the Ming Empire to circulate on the same footing as standard cash. To Counterfeit is death. The informant will receive 250 taels in silver and in addition the entire property of the criminal.' As well as being the

3 A two-kwan note of the 1263 issues by Emperor Yuan Shih Tsu. As Hu Pi Li he became Emperor of China after conquering the Sung dynasty and he ruled for 15 years. It was this type of note that was first described to the Western world by Marco Polo and other travellers

earliest available to collectors the Ming notes are also the largest banknotes, measuring 13in × 9in.

AMERICA

The New World was not slow in issuing paper money, although the British had no wish to encourage the economy of the early Americans and British governors were instructed to refuse note issues except in cases of dire emergency. This meant that paper money would only be issued by the British authorities for carrying on war, and the first issue came on 10 December, 1690 at Massachusetts Bay. This was to pay for the military expedition into Canada—'King William's War'. This was followed by another issue of paper money in South Carolina when a punitive expedition was launched against the Spaniards and the Indians entrenched in Florida. Queen Anne's war of 1702-13 managed without paper money until 1709 when New Hampshire, Connecticut, New York and New Jersey began issuing notes.

Three Shillings&fourpence

Issued in defence of American Liberty

Ense petit placidam sub Libertate, Quietem

Decm: 7.ᵗʰ 1775.

4 'Issued in defence of American Liberty' and showing the famous Minute-man armed with sword. The note was engraved and printed by Paul Revere, one of the world's greatest silversmiths and a staunch supporter of the American cause

man' (militiaman) armed with sword and the words 'Issued in Defence of American Liberty'. Others show a fish as the vignette. They are known to collectors as the 'Sword in Hand' and 'Codfish' notes respectively. Benjamin Franklin was another famous American to issue notes.

These early notes are particularly interesting because they indicate the complete break with England. In 1775 the Continental Congress began issuing its own notes and these were headed 'The United Colonies'. Two years later the famous name first appeared—'The United States'. Because the Treasury was empty the 'Continentals' had an unsuccessful circulation and the expression arose—sometimes still used today— 'Not worth a Continental'.

Many hundreds of different notes of this period can be found and they are all hand-signed, usually by several people. Because of the difficulty of getting people to accept these notes, well-known figures were persuaded to sign the notes in the hope that this would more readily permit their circulation. This has resulted in nine signatories of the Declaration of Independence, seven of the Articles of Confederation, ten of the Stamp Act Congress and eleven of the United States Constitution, being available on the early paper money.

George Washington took an interest in the paper money and preserved some examples in his personal diary. A form of paper money which is virtually unobtainable are the 'receipts' he personally signed when appropriating farmers' stocks for the use of his ill-fed army.

POLAND

All early paper money was introduced because of great emergency and Poland provides a good example of this. Banknotes of the Polish War of Independence

As the eighteenth century progressed more and more paper money appeared— in direct contravention of British orders. But few people, at that time, intended that there should be a complete break with Britain. The notes frequently referred to the King of England and were dated 'issued . . . in the reign of King George III'. The crown was often used as a vignette. But once rebellion was decided upon the notes quickly changed, propaganda replacing the crown. Perhaps the most famous notes are those engraved and printed by Paul Revere. Some of these show a 'Minute-

(1794) are today very rare but, occasionally, turn up in remarkably good condition. This is because they did not circulate for long—war overtook them and crushed ruthlessly the brave leaders of the insurrection.

The notes, beautifully produced, remain testimony to a great man of freedom, Thaddeus Kosciuszko, a man whose place in history had already been assured when he fought at the side of George Washington in the American War of Independence.

On returning to his native country he found great disorder. The death of King Sobieski without heir had been the signal for foreign intervention. Frederick the Great of Prussia brought about the first partition of Poland— by which the country lost a third of its territory.

The Poles formed a new constitution on 3 May 1791—still a Polish National Day—made the monarchy hereditary and introduced reforms which caused the Russian armies to move into Poland again.

It was in this state of turmoil that the freedom-loving Thaddeus Kosciuszko rose to lead the Polish people in the War of Independence of 1794. Unusual for any revolution, Kosciuszko had the support of rich and poor alike: noblemen and peasants flocked to his banner. There was hardly any money available to support the insurrection, so Kosciuszko issued the famous Insurrection notes.

It was not, however, a practical insurrection, though hope was given to the desperate venture on 3 April when Kosciuszko with a mixed army of peasants and regulars defeated an army of Russian veterans at the Battle of Raclawice. But he was finally defeated in a series of major battles at Szczekociny,

5 The Continental currency was the first federally issued paper money and was made to pay for the expenses of the American Revolution. This $3 bill of 1779 shows an eagle and a heron fighting. The motto translates: 'The outcome is in doubt'. The notes are named 'The United States of North America'

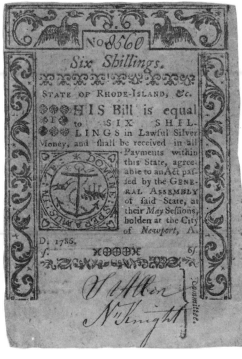

6 The famous Rhode Island issue of 1786. The legal tender provision was to be enforced by courts without trial by jury. But a lawsuit (Trevett v Weeden) resulted in the court declaring the law invalid for denying jury trial and trial by jury became a fundamental right of every United States citizen

7 Insurrection note of 1794 issued by Thaddeus Kosciuszko who succeeded in getting both noblemen and peasants to rally to his cause

notes and for the universal mortgaged National Welfare to each bearer of the actual notes, which will be accepted as well for all public revenues according to the foregoing Resolution of the Highest Council of the Nation.' The notes also bear the inscription: 'Freedom—Unity—Independence'. Denominations were in *grzywny kolonska*, which was a standard unit for assaying gold and silver in Cologne at that time.

NORWAY

Norway saw an issue of paper money in the year 1696. This was not a state issue but a private issue with a limited circulation which lasted for less than a year, when the issuer, Jorgen thor Mohlen, went bankrupt.

Mohlen, an enterprising merchant, built himself up to become the richest man in Norway, with factories producing everything from rope to gunpowder, and with ships voyaging to most parts of the world. He was unlucky in 1676 when one of his ships carrying a valuable cargo to the Guinea Coast was captured by the Dutch, and subsequently he was to lose a dozen ships to pirates and foreign powers.

His credit was seriously affected by these losses so he asked for royal permission to make an issue of paper money in 1695. Some 50,000 *krondaler* were put into circulation, Mohlen hoping that the paper money would last until his trading ships returned. But the notes were presented almost as quickly as they went into circulation. He went into bankruptcy and died in 1709.

The wording on these early notes is: 'As His Royal Majesty the 22 June this Year 1695/ his most gracious Decree has issued/ regarding certain Notes/ that shall go for Money North of the Mountains in His Royal Majesty's Kingdom

Praga and Maciejowice. On 5 November he capitulated.

The banknotes stated: '. . . which the National Treasury will pay out of the funds for backing the designated Treasury

8 Issued in 1814 at Christiania, an early Norwegian note for 16 Rigsbank skillings

9 A 24 skilling note of 1810

10 Early Swedish paper money was often on intricately watermarked paper. This note was issued in 1840—
the time the world's first adhesive postage stamps were issued in Britain

Norway/ Then is this Note according to the said Decree authorised for the value of . . . Rixdale/Croner.'

It was not until the 1700s that Copenhagen banks again ventured into the issuing of paper money but by 1810, when the Napoleonic Wars were causing a shortage of specie throughout Europe, a number of different notes had appeared.

SWEDEN

Sweden can claim the honour of issuing the first banknotes in Europe from a major bank. The instigator was Johan Palmstruch, who had first put forward the idea of a bank with circulating notes as early as 1652. These were to be called 'small bank letters' (*Banckbrieflein*) and were to be issued for round amounts, transferable by means of endorsement.

The idea was not adopted then, but in 1660 when currency depreciation caused a run on the banks and a great shortage of specie the Swedish government reviewed the situation. On 16 July 1661

the first Swedish notes appeared, drawn on the Stockholms Banco which had been founded by Palmstruch.

His notes were intended to bridge the gap between the coining of specie and the void created by the existing shortage. They were notes of credit (*kreditivsedlar*).

Professor Heckscher, Swedish economist and historian, contends that the invention of banknotes constitutes Palmstruch's claim to a place in the history of money and banking.

Other countries may have a claim to have issued paper money at much earlier dates, but the Swedish issue were banknotes, payable on demand, non interest-bearing and able to pass freely from hand to hand.

AUSTRALIA

Britain first made use of Australia by establishing a convict colony at Sydney Cove and in its earliest days this colony employed paper money because of the great shortage of coin.

11 An early note from Hobart Town dated 1835. Made out for £7 it was issued by the cashier of the Derwent Bank

12 Private paper money was popular in the pioneering days of Australia. This £1.10s. note of New South Wales was issued by Dalwood Vineyards

The Commissariat store would issue receipts for produce it bought from the early settlers and these 'store receipts' were the first paper money to be used to any extent. They were regarded as safe bills of exchange because they had government backing. Similarly the military paymasters issued 'receipts' for regimental purchases which circulated freely.

Private merchants, realising the potential of all this, soon began issuing their own 'notes'. It was not until 1817 that Australia opened its first bank, the Bank of New South Wales, but by 1840 there were over twenty different banks issuing notes.

The earliest known Australian paper currency are the issues of Garnham Blaxcell in 1814. Blaxcell and his partners, D'Arcy Wentworth and Alexander Riley, undertook to build Sydney Hospital for the right to import 60,000 gallons of rum in four years. Blaxcell issued notes on the strength of this and they became the principal currency in Sydney despite an order from Governor Macquarie that duties must be paid in sterling, Spanish dollars or Commissariat bills.

CANADA

Canada also owed its first use of paper money to war with Britain. The French, pressed hard by Britain's warships, had difficulty in supplying their colony and in 1685 the French governor, Vaudreuil, issued notes.

But he did something quite unusual— he issued playing cards as money, taking the view that they were strong and would last well. Dated 1714 these first playing card notes are signed by the governor and Intendant Bregon. The issues were reasonably successful and later issues were made on ordinary card until the French authority was replaced by Britain in 1759.

SOUTH AFRICA

When war broke out between Britain and the Netherlands the British navy had such a command of the sea that the Dutch found it very difficult to get through to the Cape of Good Hope.

When the supply of coins dried up in 1782 the Dutch Governor, Van Plettenberg, issued paper money to offset the shortage. These early notes are in *rixdollar* and *stiver* denominations. The Cape of Good Hope had no printing press so the notes were all handwritten and this practice continued until 1803 when printing presses were used in South Africa for the first time.

13 Colonial *treasury note* issued at Quebec in 1753 for 48 livres

14 An unissued note from Montagu Bank, Cape of Good Hope. Nineteenth-century notes of South Africa are all very scarce

2: British Notes

The goldsmiths, considered by many historians 'the fathers of British banking', were the first to set up in England a system of paper money which, in London at least, enjoyed a general circulation among the moneyed classes. There had, of course, been earlier payment documents like the Military Payment Certificate dated 14 March 1635 to Sir Francis Godolphin, but the goldsmith's note could be used from hand to hand— it was a running cash note, a name that the Bank of England was to use for its own issues later on.

The banking power of the goldsmiths came about when Charles I seized the treasure in the Tower of London in 1640 in order to carry on the Civil War. The nobility and merchants had been accustomed to depositing their gold and silver in the Tower for safekeeping. They now looked for safer deposit systems and found goldsmiths willing bankers.

The goldsmiths already had vaults to protect their own valuable wares and they issued receipts which represented actual gold and silver. It was therefore easy for merchants to use such receipts in business transactions.

The goldsmith notes were endorsed from hand to hand as they circulated and, as early as 1677, one writer advocated that such notes should be able to pass without the necessity of endorsement. Then, in 1692, a goldsmith's note became the subject of a court case (Buller *v* Crips) and Lord Holt ruled that it was illegal and could not be transferred. It was not until 1704 that English promissory notes were officially given the same rights as bills of exchange. Lord Holt's decision was later to be reversed by the Lord Chief Justice of England who pronounced it 'a blot on our judicial history'.

Exchequer orders were the first 'notes'

July 1st 1676

I Promise to pay to Mr Thomas Percivall or the bearer hereof on demand and delivery of this note the sums of One hundred Pounds

£ 100 —

For my . . . Sir Robt Clayton & John Morris Esq.

pp Deane Monteage

MONTEAGE, Deane, 1676.

to enjoy the full status of legal tender. This was an order to the Teller of the Receipt of the Exchequer to pay such and such a person so much out of the fund of a Parliamentary supply. Where the exchequer order represented the repayment of a loan it bore interest.

The Bank of England was established in 1694 and at that time very few people had any inkling that it was to become the great pivot of the British economy that it is today. Indeed it was founded by a form of trickery. The subscribers of the money for William's war would be trustees and 'their bills of property should be current', the group being ready 'as a Bank to exchange such current Bills the better to give Credit thereto, and make the said Bills the better to circulate' (*Journal of the House of Commons*).

Lord Macaulay was later to comment: 'It was not easy to guess that a Bill which purported only to impose a new duty on tonnage for the benefit of such persons as should advance money towards carrying on the war, was really a Bill creating the greatest commercial institution that the World has ever seen.'

Even so, the Bank's paper money did not enjoy the status of legal tender and it was not until 1833 that limited legal tender status was granted. It may come as a surprise to many people to know that the famous Bank of England £1 was not legal tender until 1928!

No time was lost in introducing paper money by the Bank of England. The first 'Court' met on 27 July 1694 and decided upon three types of note, all of which were in use by the goldsmith bankers of the day.

15 One of the earliest known drawn notes — dated 1676. It reads: 'I promise to pay to Mr Thomas Percivall or the bearer hereof on demand and delivery of this note the sums of one hundred pounds . For my . . .Sir Robt Clayton and John Morris Esq. pp Deane Monteage.'

16 An early bill of exchange for £200 dated 1663 (though possibly in error for 1662). It reads: 'For Mr John Morris and Mr Clayton at ye Flying Horse in Cornhill. Pay to Mr Richard Drake ye summe of two hundred pounds upon ye account of Robert Guyder'. The note is endorsed: 'Rec'd ye 8 January 1663 according to the order of this bill two hundred pounds (£200) Richard Drake.'

There were to be running cash notes, the forerunners of our modern banknotes. These notes could be used in part, the amount withdrawn being endorsed on the note. This was later to allow a collector to cash an early Bank of England note for its full amount less one penny, retaining the note as his receipt for the deposit of 1d.

There were also accomptable notes, the forerunners of cheques (cheque books were introduced about 1830). These were certificates of deposit and gave the depositor the right to 'draw notes' on the Bank of England. Such withdrawals were endorsed on the accomptable note. Later, special forms were prepared by the Bank of England with a 'check' pattern. Drawn notes were written by depositors on these forms which thus became an early version of the modern cheque.

The other method of 'note issue' was the sealed bills, which can be likened to the present deposit book system. These were not banknotes in the strict sense as they were promissory notes, normally bearing interest and issued against deposits or pledged assets. If they were intended to circulate from hand to hand they were not successful and within twenty years went out of use altogether.

However, they have the distinction of being the very first note issues of the Bank of England. On 1 August 1694 sealed bills in amounts of £100 each and bearing an interest rate of 2d a day, were issued to people nominated by the Treasury. They were, of course, the promised payments to enable the King to carry on the war with France, and for which they were permitted to establish a bank. Over eleven thousand notes were issued, the majority to Lord Ranelagh (for the Army) and Anthony Stevens (for the Navy).

A few of the notched wooden tallies given by the Exchequer as receipts for this money can still be seen in the Bank's historical collection. John Kenrick was the 'First Cashier'.

Part printed notes were not introduced until 1696. In 1695 the Bank of Scotland was established and this Bank has the distinction of issuing the first £1 note (1699)—a note for twenty shillings. The Bank of England did not introduce £1 notes until 1797.

It is ironical that although today the

bankers of the United Kingdom are held to be of the highest integrity, the early bankers indulged in business methods that were open to criticism.

Forgery

In thirty-two years more than 600 people were hanged for forging banknotes, the directors of the Bank of England prosecuting the majority of them. When the death sentence was abolished for forgery it was to the credit of the Bank of England. They applied to the Secretary of State for guilty forgers to be allowed to take their families with them to Botany Bay, and on occasion made payments of money so that the families were not penniless on the journey to Australia. The last recorded execution for forgery of a banknote took place in Glasgow in September 1821. The victim was a woman, Anne Wilson, who had been found guilty of uttering a forged note.

Today it is an offence knowingly to possess a forged banknote and the penalties can be severe. But in the 1800s the law was not over-much concerned with 'knowingly' possessing forged notes; just being caught in possession of one was enough and the minimum penalty was transportation. The more usual penalty was a public hanging. By this time charges of forgery were so commonplace that juries began to bring in verdicts of 'not guilty' against the clearest of evidence, because of the severity of the punishment.

That someone who by ill-chance received forged notes could be hanged worried the consciences of many people, and the Society of Arts published a book in 1819, 'Report on the Mode of Preventing the Forgery of Banknotes', in an attempt to remedy the situation. The Society of Arts condemned the

Bank of England for not taking sufficient trouble to make their notes unimitable and proposed a banknote which would defeat the forger.

In their foreword the society stated: 'The increasing reluctance of Juries to visit with the extreme penalty of the law, a crime, for the prevention of which no successful precautions have apparently been taken, and the notorious fact, corroborated by evidence produced at several recent trials, that forged notes have passed undetected through the scrutiny of the Bank Inspectors, have attracted general attention.'

Notes were at the time produced from copper plates which would each account for about 6,000. With a daily issue of small notes in excess of 30,000, this meant a daily consumption of five plates and a total of 1,500 a year. The society proposed that steel plates should be used, and that only superior artists should be employed.

It must be remembered that at this time copperplate letter writing was a large industry and many people were able to make perfect facsimiles. J. T. Barber Beaumont, addressing the Society of Arts said:

17 The Bank of England first introduced £1 notes in 1797. Until 1826 they were printed in the same style as the white £5 notes

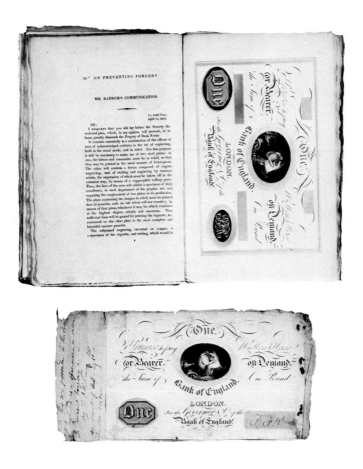

forgeries, some should be desperate enough to commit them. Now if, instead of being the common-place work of inferior writing engravers (who are so numerous) bank note plates were masterpieces of the best historical engravers (who are few), whose talent is so rarely to be found, the number of persons who would be able to attempt an imitation with any chance of success, would be very inconsiderable indeed—not ten persons, perhaps, where there are now ten thousand.

T. C. Hansard provided the society with the details of cost for the steel plate production of notes which amounted to £1,500 to £2,000 and would take at least twelve months to bring to perfection . . . 'but after that, with the expense of six or seven thousand pounds more, to perfect the presses and other apparatus, the production will be so rapid, and at so little cost, that the savings of a few months will defray the whole expense of the preparations, and then the notes will be produced at the cost of half a farthing each'.

T. Ransom produced the suggested plate for an unimitable note, which was submitted to the Bank of England.

It consists essentially in a combination of the efforts of men of acknowledged celebrity in the art of engraving, both in the usual mode, and in relief. For this purpose it will be necessary to make use of two steel plates: in one, the letters and ornaments must be in relief, so that they may be printed in the usual manner of letter-press. The other will contain a device composed of engine engraving, and of etching and engraving by eminent artists, the impression of which must be taken off in the common way, by means of a copper-plate rolling press. Thus, the face of the note will exhibit a specimen of high excellence, in each depart-

18 The Society of Arts published a book in 1819 dealing with the prevention of forgery. The illustration shows the actual specimen submitted to the Bank of England by the society as being a design which would be much harder to forge than existing notes. In slightly altered form it was also reproduced in the book

Forgeries of Bank of England notes are so frequent because they are so easy of imitation. They are of inferior workmanship to common engraved shop-bills. An apprentice to a writing engraver of two years standing, by three or four days work, is able to copy a bank note plate, so that ordinary judges cannot tell the genuine from the spurious. There are not less than 10,000 persons in this country who are able to engrave successful imitations of Bank of England notes, and nine-tenths of these are in needy, and many of them in distressed circumstances. It is, therefore, not surprising, if amongst so many who are competent to relieve their necessities by these

ment of the graphic art, and requiring the employment of two plates in its production . . .

The Bank of England remained impassive.

The book contained the opinions of many other interested parties and covered the detail of banknote production to the extent of showing designs for the printing presses. It had little or no effect on the directors of the Bank of England and people continued to hang. But the seeds of reform had been sown, and in 1819 the famous artist (and reformer) George Cruikshank caused such a stir with his 'anti-hanging note' that he succeeded where many eminent minds had failed. Hanging for possessing forged banknotes, together with hanging for all minor offences, was abolished for good.

In his own words, George Cruikshank describes what happened:

Fifty-eight years back from this date (1876), there were 'one pound' Bank of England notes in circulation and unfortunately, many forged notes were in circulation also, or being 'passed', the punishment for which offence was in some cases transportation, in others death. At this period, having to go early one morning to the Royal Exchange, I passed Newgate Jail and saw several persons suspended from the gibbet, two of these were women who had been executed for passing one pound forged notes.

I determined if possible to put a stop to such terrible punishment for such a crime, and made a sketch of the above note, and then an etching of it.

Mr Hone published it, and it created a sensation. The Directors of the Bank of England were exceedingly wrath.

19 The Cruickshank anti-hanging note which played an important part in legislation to abolish hanging for all minor offences

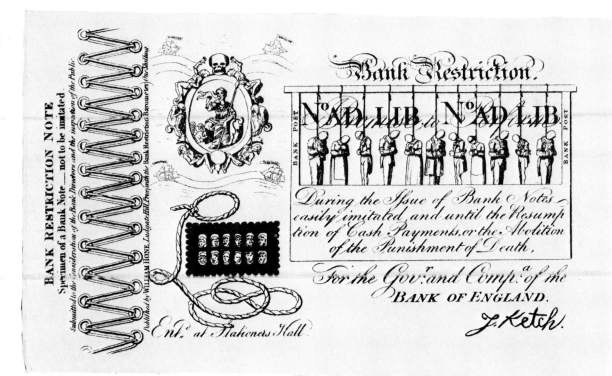

The crowd round Hone's shop in Ludgate Hill was so great that the Lord Mayor had to send the police to clear the street. The notes were in such demand that they could not be printed fast enough, and I had to sit up all one night to etch another plate. Mr Hone realised above £700 and I had the satisfaction of knowing that no man or woman was ever hanged after this for passing one-pound forged Bank of England notes.

The issue of my 'Bank Note not to be Imitated' not only put a stop to the issue of any more Bank of England one pound notes, but also put a stop to the punishment of death for such an offence—not only for that, but likewise, for forgery—and then the late Sir Robert Peel revised the Penal Code; so that the final effect of my note was to stop the hanging for all minor offences, and has thus been the means of saving thousands of men and women from being hanged.

Strangely enough the Bank of England has itself been concerned with the forgery of notes, albeit with government sanction! They were at least part responsible for the forgery in large numbers of French *assignats* during the French Revolution. And while the forgery of

British notes by the Germans in World War II is well known, it is also a fact that the British forged German notes—to the extent of putting rude poems about Adolf Hitler on the backs of German military paper money.

Forged banknotes are now retained by the Bank of England. An unusual situation arose over a note when in 1818 an engraver called Ransom was accused of passing a forged note to a Mr Mitchener. The Bank of England had retained the note when presented by Mitchener. Not unnaturally Mitchener went to Ransom to get his money back. Ransom demanded the note and an inspector from the Bank of England produced the note. Ransom immediately pocketed the note whereupon the inspector, a Mr Fish, had him imprisoned to await trial for possessing a forged note. But for some reason best known to the Bank of England they did not turn up at the court to prove the note was a forgery and Ransom was acquitted. He immediately sued Fish and obtained £100 damages for wrongful imprisonment.

THE PRESENTATION OF NOTES

It is a true and proud boast of the Bank of England that they will honour and redeem any note which they have ever issued. But note-holders in the Napoleonic days were not always so happy with the Bank of England. The value of notes depreciated and at one time £1 notes actually sold for 15s. Instances are known where a Bank of England £1 had to be exchanged with 5s in silver for a gold sovereign.

In Scotland bankers behaved in a most ungentlemanly manner towards one another on occasions. The Bank of

20 Many beautiful essays were produced for Bank of England £1 notes

Scotland, which had started out life with a complete monopoly, made the mistake of forgetting to apply for an extension of that monopoly and before they realised what had happened, were confronted with the establishment of the Royal Bank of Scotland. The two banks set about trying to destroy each other. Their method was simply to save up as many of the other banks' notes as possible and then suddenly present them for payment.

This led to the 'option clause' on banknotes, a typical example being the wording of the Royal Bank of Scotland's notes: 'One pound sterling on demand, Or in the Option of the Directors, one pound six pence sterling at the end of six months after the day of the demand . . .'

Because of a serious shortage of specie in the mid-eighteenth century, the Scottish banks were forced to issue optional notes again. In an effort to preserve its silver coin, the Royal Bank of Scotland issued the first Scottish guinea note in 1758. The last of the guinea notes were printed in 1828, their issue finally being forbidden by the Bank Notes (Scotland) Act of 1845, which declared notes containing fractions of a £1 illegal.

Attempts to cause trouble by presentation of notes in large quantities were often met with dubious practices. An agent employed to collect and present such quantity of notes to Murdoch & Co, found that after 34 days standing at the tellers desk he had only received in payment money for £2,893 of the notes. Murdoch's simply paid out day by day in sixpences. Mr Trotter, the agent, recorded:

When their notes were presented at the office for payment, a Bag of Sixpences was with great deliberation produced and laid upon the table; the

Teller then proceeded with ridiculous slowness to open up the bag and count the money. He would first tell over a pound sterling, in single sixpences ranked upon the table, and then affecting to be uncertain about the reckoning, he would gather this small money, and count it over again from one hand to the other, sometimes letting fall a sixpence for a pretence to begin anew and count it over again; on other occasions he would make time by ridiculous discourses upon the odd size or shape of particular sixpences, sound another upon the table, to try if it was sufficient coin. And sometimes he would quit his occupation altogether upon the pretence of some sudden errand or call out of the room. Very often they employed one Coggill, by his ordinary occupation a Porter, to act the Teller, and he lost time and blundered with great alacrity—being instructed to do his worst.

Mr Trotter went to the lengths of having a notary and two witnesses attend such a pay out, but Coggill was still set to work in the usual way. People of lesser importance were sometimes

21 Stornaway was a powerful bank in the early 1800s but was one of the few in Scotland which went into bankruptcy

treated with considerable roughness by the tellers and at least on one occasion a man received a beating as well as payment in sixpences!

The Bank of England was more subtle in its approach to such problems as a run on the bank. They would pay out in sixpences, laboriously counted, but would employ people to join the queues for payment so that they could draw the money out and then re-deposit it at another window. The Bank of England ceased to issue £1 notes in 1826, and did not re-issue them again until 1928.

Robbery by highwaymen seriously worried the Bank of England because the postboys were easy prey for robbers, the system of well-guarded mail coaches not coming in until near the end of the eighteenth century. To offset this they instituted a system of promissory notes payable at three days' sight (1724). It

22 An unissued note of the Gloucestershire Banking Company which in 1885 united with Capital and Counties Bank Ltd

was also a practice to cut notes in half and send them by different coaches to be rejoined at their destination. This also happened in World War II when notes were returned from the Middle East.

The most perilous moment in the Bank's history came with the Gordon Riots, when, on 6 June 1780, Lord George Gordon headed a vast mob which raided Newgate Prison and then attacked the Bank of England. Only the timely intervention of the military saved the Bank, and from that date onwards the Brigade of Guards has furnished a 'Bank Guard'.

PRIVATE BANKS

Although the Bank of England enjoyed a monopoly of note-issues within a 65 mile radius of London there was still plenty of scope for private banks. The goldsmith bankers had flourished and private banking was building up

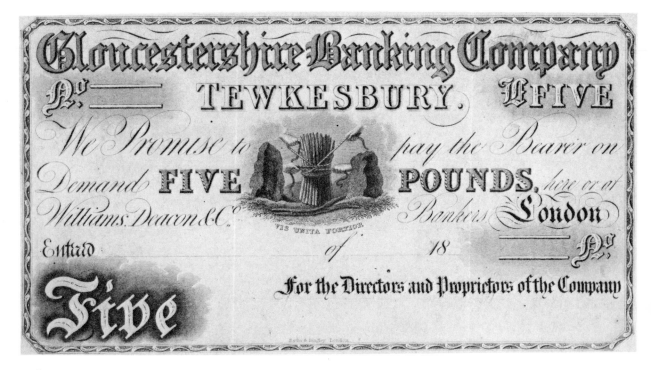

Twenty Shillings · Dunbar · 1 Nov.ʳ 1821

THE EAST LOTHIAN Banking Comp.ᵃ Promise to pay _____ or Bearer on Demand One Pound Sterling At their Office here By Order of the Directors

when the South Sea Bubble burst in 1720. Banking was retarded from then on because of the Jacobite claims and Prince Charles's march into England swept away a number of country banks. Edmund Burke told the House of Commons that when he came to London in 1750 there 'were not twelve country banks in the whole of England'.

But from 1750 private banks flourished, and issued notes in all kinds of denominations—even for such sums as 5½d; and in Scotland notes appeared for 1d. Skit notes for 1d even contained an 'option clause'! Such a note, bordered by drawings of wasps' reads:

I, John Bragg, cashier for Andrew Whitecock, Duncan Dick and Company, Bankers in Glasgow, having powers from them, promise to pay to Thomas Tailor or the bearer on demand ONE PENNY, sterling, or in option of the directors Three ballads, six days after demand, and for ascertaining the demand and option of the directors, the acquaintant and one of the tellers of the bank are hereby ordered to mark and sign this note on the back hereof. By order of the Court Directors.

It must be remembered that few people could read and write and such notes caused considerable confusion. From time to time economic disruptions caused banks to fail, and on one severe occasion, in 1772, 525 private banks in England went into bankruptcy.

At one time there were more than 900 private banks issuing notes. Many of these banks have quite extraordinary histories behind them. The East Lothian Bank,

23 Borthwick, who signed this note, absconded with much of the bank's capital and was never caught

for example, started in 1810 with a capital of £80,000. Its notes circulated more than any others in Haddingtonshire until 1822 when it suddenly went out of business. The reason was that the Chief Cashier, William Borthwick, disappeared with much of the bank's capital and was never traced.

Borthwick had been misappropriating the bank's money for sometime, furthering the business adventures of his relatives in the shipping business. When it became apparent that certain directors were becoming suspicious, he laid plans to have them placed in large puncheons (whisky barrels) and shipped from Dundee to Danzig from where they were to be taken to Prussia. He was never able to implement the plan and had to flee. Directors searched for him in America and Norway without success. Even so the bank's creditors were paid in full and Sir William Forbes helped by retiring their notes amounting to more than £50,000.

Few private banks rival in interest the affairs of Jonathan Backhouse & Co. This was one of the original 20 banks which joined together to form the nucleus of Barclays Bank as it is known today. Its notes are therefore still valid. John Edward Mounsey of that bank became one of the first directors of Barlcays and was made local director in 1914.

The Backhouse family were linen and worsted manufacturers and were doing banking business before they started a separate bank. Jonathan's father had been appointed Agent of the Royal Exchange Assurance in 1759.

The firm was established in 1774 as Backhouse & Co, the name changing to Jonathan Backhouse & Co in 1798. It amalgamated with Barclays in 1896. Notes of the bank were forged as early as 1778 and £100 was offered at that time for the apprehension and conviction of forgers. One, at least, was subsequently hanged.

24 Jonathan Backhouse was perhaps one of the most colourful bankers of his day. A staunch Quaker he had a great sense of humour and was to become one of the directors of Barclays Bank

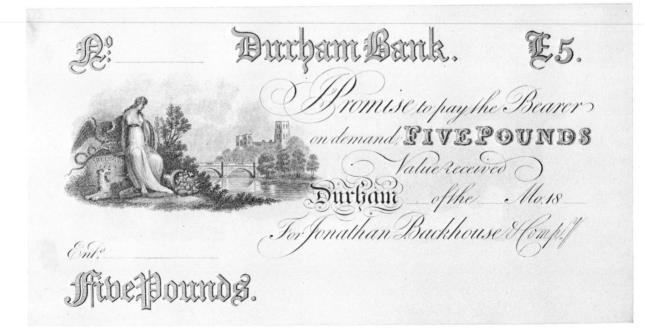

The bank was established at Darlington and Lord Darlington attempted to 'break the bank' by instructing all his tenants to pay rent in Backhouse notes. He intended to accumulate these notes and present them, hoping to put the banker in a position where he could not pay his own notes. But Jonathan Backhouse heard of this and sent to London for a large supply of bullion which he rushed back to Darlington. As the chaise was passing through Croft a front wheel came off the vehicle. Rather than wait for the wheel to be replaced, such was the hurry, he balanced the cash in the back and drove on at speed on three wheels. Lord Darlington's agent duly presented a large parcel of notes which were paid promptly in gold, Backhouse remarking: 'Now tell thy master that if he will sell Raby I will pay for it with the same metal.'

The bank records confirm these affairs: 1819 25th—To bank and cash to London £32,000.

31 of 7th mo—(profit and loss account debited £2. 3s) wheel demolished.

Maberly Phillips records another amusing incident relating to a commercial traveller:

It so happened that one of these gentlemen, after having dined freely at the King's Head, Barnard Castle, was boasting to a company present in the Commercial room of his own importance. Jonathan Backhouse, attired in the usual dress of the Society of Friends, unknown to the rest of the company, was in the room, quietly reading his newspaper when he was attacked by the wealthy commercial, and, by a series of sarcastic remarks, held up to ridicule as a man out of harmony. The traveller offered to bet £5 that Backhouse could not produce as much money. Mr. Backhouse, after a great deal of banter, said he did not bet, but to show his indifference to money offered to put a £5 note in the fire if the traveller would do the same. Backhouse took out a £5 note and put it in the fire. The commercial,

25 *A specimen from the Barclay and Fry Archives of a £10 note of the Grantham Bank*

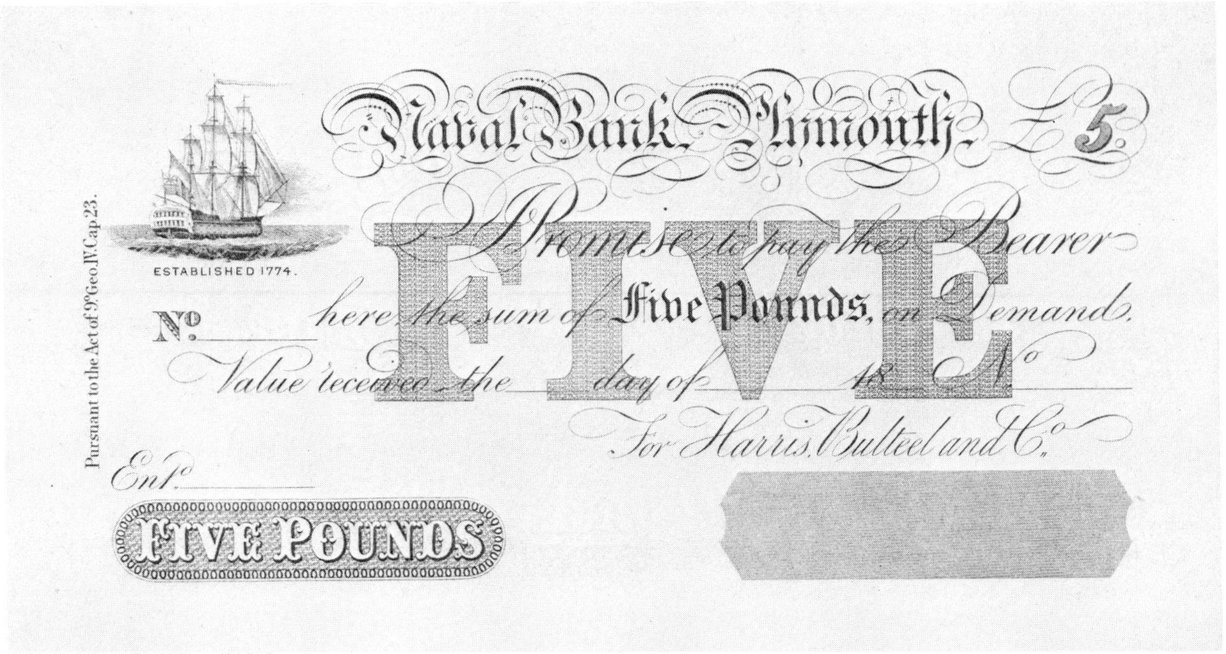

26 A very rare example of a
£5 note of the Naval Bank,
Plymouth

27 Tring, Aylesbury and Chesham Bank was among the
many nineteenth century banks which begun using two colours
on their notes

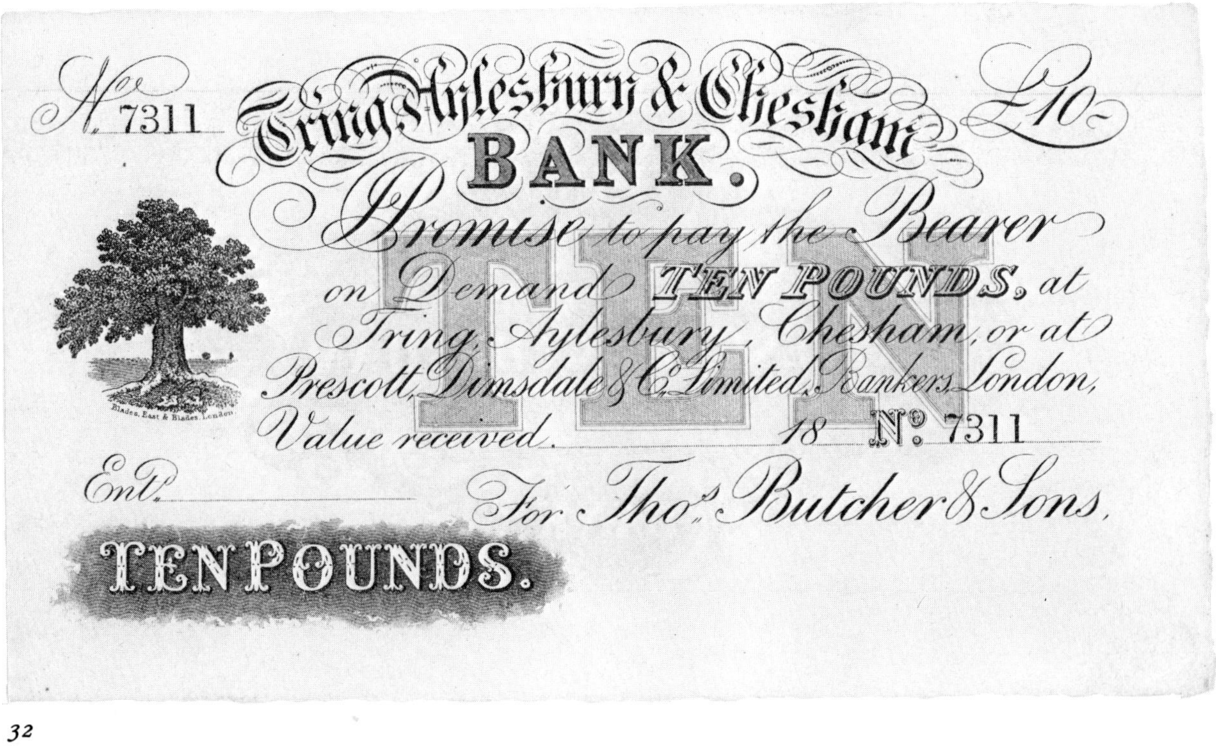

not wishing to be behind, did the same. Mr. Backhouse offered to repeat the process but the commercial, considerably cowed, declined. Mr. Backhouse quietly thanked him for having burned one of his (Backhouse) bank notes for which he received £5, while the note he, Mr. Backhouse, had burned, was on his own bank, and had only cost him the paper.

28 £1 Treasury note printed on stamp watermarked paper and rushed through at the beginning of the Great War when a shortage of specie was expected

The Crisis of World War I

If private banks had their problems for survival, The Bank of England also had worries in time of international crisis. The Great War of 1914-18 saw a serious financial position for the Bank of England. The Governor, Walter Cunliffe, reported that the 'financial and trading interests in the city were totally opposed to our intervening in the war'. Within five days the Bank of England paid out over £27 million and the reserve fell to less than £1 million. The possibility loomed of the Bank not being able to meet demands.

In July of 1914 the Bank of England presented to the Government a design for a £1 note in anticipation of trouble. But the Treasury did not think the Bank of England would have sufficient time to implement it and went ahead with their own notes. The August Bank Holiday was extended for three clear days to allow the Treasury to rush through the printing of the notes. At the time there were not sufficient stocks of banknote paper so the Treasury used stamp paper. The first issue of Treasury notes bears the Royal Cypher 'simple' watermark as do the postage stamps of the period. Another step taken to offset the expected shortage of money was to make postal orders legal tender.

The printers of the Treasury notes, Waterlow and Sons, were only given three days to produce the notes. They suc-

ceeded, but the quality was very poor. In October the design was changed to a more carefully engraved design. The ten shilling note came a week after the Treasury £1 notes, and these too were changed to the better designed notes in January of 1915. A third issue of Treasury Notes was made in 1917 and these showed, for the first time, the Houses of Parliament on the reverse. All these notes bore the facsimile signature of Sir John Bradbury, permanent secretary to the Treasury. He was followed by Sir Warren Fisher and, despite continual protests from the Bank of England that the notes issued should devolve into their hands, Treasury notes continued until November 1928. Then, once again, the Bank of England took over and issued their own notes, at the same time accepting responsibility for Treasury notes.

29 The Channel Islands also had many early issues of paper money, some of them extremely attractive. This note is from St Mary's Parochial Bank in Jersey. It was produced on special Jersey watermarked paper

3: The French Revolution

The French Revolution, in its effect on society, surpassed all earlier revolutions and its influence on the modern history of Europe is still felt. It might well be argued that paper money played a prominent part in sowing the seeds for revolution.

To notaphilists the French Revolution means 'assignats'—paper money backed by land instead of gold and silver. Assigning paper to land instead of metal was revolutionary in concept, staggering in its potential and catastrophic in its result. To understand the assignat properly we must take a look at the man who conceived it nearly 100 years before the French Revolution.

Surprisingly he was not a Frenchman, but a Scot. Incredibly, he was a gambler, an adventurer and a criminal. His name was John Law and he was destined to control the financial world of Europe for nearly five months in 1720. He touched off a financial mania that inflamed Europe and he gave the world the word 'millionaire' which, though now familiar both in the French and English languages, was first used to describe the Mississippian who suddenly grew rich through Law's financial intrigues.

Although rare, the banknotes issued by John Law—particularly those dated 1720—are still available and mark the beginning, 'the penny black', of any collection setting out to illustrate the paper money of the French Revolution.

John Law was born in Edinburgh in 1671, the son of a goldsmith. At this time, well before the establishment of the Bank of England, many goldsmiths acted as bankers. Ever since Charles I had confiscated the plate deposited in the Tower of London, merchants had turned more and more to the goldsmiths. The receipt notes issued by

No.º 40155 44   *Dix livres Tournois.*

Divifion

LA BANQUE promet payer au Porteur à vüe Dix livres Tournois en Efpeces d'Argent, valeur reçüe. A Paris le premier Juillet mil fept cens vingt.

Vû p.ʳ le S.ʳ Fenellon.   Signé p.ʳ le S.ʳ Bourgeois.
Giraudeau.   *Délanauze.*

                             Controllé p.ʳ le S.ʳ Dureveft.
                              Granet.

goldsmiths were readily accepted in trade because they represented actual gold and silver. Soon the goldsmiths issued notes for fixed amounts and thus acted as bankers. So John Law grew up in an atmosphere of early banking. He was educated at Edinburgh and quickly showed an amazing aptitude for mathematics, particularly algebra.

When his father died John Law went to London. He had a pleasing manner which won him many friends and he built up a reputation for his skill as a gambler and for his love affairs. One of these affairs got out of hand and resulted in a duel with a Mr Wilson. John Law killed his opponent and there followed a trial for murder. Law was convicted and sentenced to be hanged. In those days there was truly one law for the rich and one for the poor. Money talked and John Law knew better than most how to use it. He obtained a commutation of sentence and escaped to the Continent. His many adventures in Europe are detailed in George Oudard's book, *The Amazing Life of John Law.*

In 1700 Law returned to Scotland. It was here, in his native land, that John Law first proposed the use of land-money. He said: 'Wealth depends on commerce, and commerce depends on circulation'. The Scots had very little silver or gold and therefore they were poor. They needed banks which could create paper money to provide the stimulus of circulation. He claimed he would make the fields of Fife blossom with prosperity, and make the shopkeeper of Edinburgh the same as the merchant prince of Genoa and Amsterdam.

He denounced the prevailing theory that a nation's wealth rested in its stock of precious metals and said that gold and silver fluctuated like corn. But land, he said, was steady in value, intrinsically beneficial and always needed. He said: 'What I propose is to make a land currency equal to the value of the land and to the value of the actual coined money without being subject, as is coined money, to a fall in value'.

He went on to propose that commissioners should be appointed to make issue of paper money to anyone who wanted it, the paper money to be secured by mortgage to the value of two thirds of the land, or issued to the complete value if the land was surrendered to the commission. Law contended that a currency based on land would regulate itself, like a safety valve. When a man needed money and had land he could get it; when no one needed money there would be no demand and none would be issued. The details of his system were set out in his famous treatise, 'Money and Trade Considered with a Proposal for Supplying the Nation with Money'.

But he chose a poor field in which to sow his assignats! The Scots had had enough of speculation and gambles. Too many of them had jumped at the scheme for colonising the Isthmus of Darien, proposed by no less a person than the founder of the Bank of England, William Peterson. Shares in the Scottish Company of Africa and India had been avidly taken up and its own paper money issues competed with the Bank of Scotland to such an extent that the Bank of Scotland was put in a precarious position. But the system had failed and two hundred thousand Scots were poorer for it. But for the disaster the Scots might well have tried Law's scheme and we would have witnessed the issue of assignats nearly a hundred years before the French Revolution.

John Law turned his attention to France. Perhaps it was because the Scots had refused his land-money idea, perhaps because he no longer believed it would work himself—but for some reason he did not advance the idea again. Instead he offered other financial schemes and he found a ready ear in the Duke of Orleans, who had become Regent of France. The two men were already acquainted for they had met years earlier in a gambling den and the Duke of Orleans had obviously been impressed with Law's financial genius.

France was in financial distress and when Law offered to restore the commerce, build up her industries and bring glory to the duke's name he received a regent's welcome. Whether the Regent was grasping at straws in France's distress, or was carried away with the magnetism of Law's personality we shall never know. 'What is needed is credit', said Law. 'The credit that I propose to establish will be different in its nature from the kinds of credit now in general use; it will be suited to this monarchy and the present state of affairs.'

His proposals boiled down to the introduction of a bank. Banks were, at that time, unknown to France. The Bank of Amsterdam was regarded as a mystery and the Bank of England, which had opened a few years earlier, had received a lot of opposition from the so-called practical and hard-headed businessmen of the day. Law claimed: 'A State must have a certain quantity of money proportioned to the number of its people.' The money he intended to create was to be secured by commercial credit. In fact this was not an original idea, it was really an extension of the English goldsmith's system, but Law now put the theory forward on a national scale.

When the charter came before the Council of Finance, Law found himself up against strong intellectual opposition. This came mainly from Saint-Simon, a hidebound old member of the aristocracy and a member of the Council of the Regency. Saint-Simon's memoirs give a vivid account of the council's deliberations and his own objections. He saw two major dangers. The first was the difficulty in directing the bank with sufficient skill to avoid the over-issue of notes. The second was that while such a bank might be safe under the government of a republic or a limited monarchy, France had an absolute monarchy and so the system was sure to be abused sooner or later. An expensive war or even an extravagant mistress could soon exhaust such a bank.

If Saint-Simon's memoirs are to be believed then John Law showed little sagacity in replying to these criticisms. But he remained adamant that the system would work and claimed that the system would so increase the wealth of France and at the same time the revenue of the King, that it was incredible to suppose that any monarch would destroy such a valuable asset.

In the face of such opposition the best Law could obtain from the Council was a charter for a private bank which was granted on 2 May 1716. In June the bank opened and was known as the Banque Generale. It was really rather humble, the bank opening in the house where Law lived in the Place Louis le Grand.

But the astute Law issued his first notes redeemable in coin of a fixed weight. This brought immediate success to the bank. Previously the money had been subjected by the government to so many modifications that it fluctuated like shares. Law's new notes were safe, they were not subject to sudden changes in value by a royal edict, and this meant that business relations abroad opened with renewed vigour. Interest rates on good paper dropped from 30 per cent to 6 per cent and later to 4 per cent. Money-lenders closed their shops and in October

31 Handsigned John Law note of 1720 for 100 livres

No. 1 8 3 8 4 7 7   Cent livres Tournois.

LA BANQUE promet payer au Porteur à vüe Cent livres Tournois en Efpeces d'Argent, valeur reçeüe. A Paris le premier Janvier mil fept cens vingt.

Vû p.r le S.r Fenellon.

Signé p.r le S.r Bourgeois.

Contrôllé p.r le S.r Durevest.

1716 tax collectors were instructed to pay these notes on sight when presented. This in effect made Law's private bank-notes legal tender. As the Banque Generale prospered the Regent took less notice of his council and gave Law new powers. It is even said that Peter the Great of Russia made an approach to Law to reorganise his finances. In 1718 the Banque Generale was converted into a state bank, the Banque Royale.

John Law proposed developing French colonial possessions on the basis of his credit. Elgin Groseclose wrote of this:

He drew up and presented to the Regent his scheme for his Mississippi Company which would enjoy extensive monopolistic privileges in Louisiana. Louisiana was then but a name, an unknown territory of unknown extent in which the claims of the French government were staked out by a few scattered forts and trading posts. When the extent and the present wealth of this territory is considered, we cannot but admire the audacity of imagination of the man who could conceive the gigantic enterprise of colonising it, or fail to excuse the enthusiasm to which he succumbed or the wild speculation which arose over the prospects for the development of this area.

The Duke of Orleans supported him all the way and to Law's powers were added the tobacco monopoly of France, other development companies, the privilege of coinage, and the monopoly of the tax farm.

As Law progressed so he seemed to think bigger and bigger. Now he proposed nothing less than the vast conversion of the national debt, offering to advance the state some 1,500 million livres at 3 per cent, intending to raise this sum by the sale of shares in the company.

Law persuaded prominent people to buy shares in order to attract the attention of general buyers; he even took an option himself on shares at a price 200 livres above the market and deposited 40,000 livres as security. As a stock-jobbing operation it ranked as one of the major coups of history. The public bought eagerly.

Cunningly Law now required subscribers to his new shares to be holders of certain numbers of the old shares. This had the effect of raising the value of the old shares. The new shares were called *filles* (daughters), and before Law had finished he had *meres* (mothers) and even grand-daughters. In 40 days share values rose by 100 per cent. In July 1719 original shares of 500 livres were quoted at 1,000; by September they were 5,000.

To support all this Law used the printing press to create Banque Royale notes. In the spring of 1719 there were 100 million livres outstanding, by July 300 million, and during the last few months of 1719 800 million livres were issued. When in July there was an incipient run on the bank, Law took the audacious step of actually lowering the value of gold.

The Rue Quincampoix had been used by men dealing in government obligations and the speculation now saw events in the Rue Quincampoix that have no parallel in history. There were no broker's offices and share dealing was done in the highway. Thirty thousand foreigners were in Paris in 1719 in search of a fortune. Stagecoach seats to the city were so much in demand that they had to be paid for months in advance. Those who could not afford to gamble on the Rue Quincampoix contented themselves with speculation on seats in the stagecoaches.

As much as 20,000 livres were paid for a single share of which the par value was 500. With the discount of bills of state, 20,000 livres put into these shares at the end of 1718 would have netted 2 million a year later. A valet was said to have made fifty million, a bootblack forty, and a restaurant waiter thirty. The word 'millionaire' came into being.

When Law visited this street he received the acclamation usually reserved for a sovereign. His native town of Edinburgh sent him the freedom of the city addressed to 'The Right Honourable John Law'. The English Ambassador in France was not on friendly terms with John Law and for this reason he was recalled. The head of the House of Stuart, pretender to the English throne, wrote to Law for his advice.

The climax of his success was that on 5 January 1720 Law was made Comptroller General of France. The inevitable happened. Early in November large blocks of stock were put on to the market. The value of the banknotes began to drop. Law introduced measures to bolster them, including an official premium of 5 per cent over coin, and on 11 March the use of gold or silver for the payment of any debt was forbidden.

France, to this day, holds the distinction of having once been the only civilised country in the world where a man could not pay his debts by gold or silver. But this was a departure from the principles of Law's bank. Things went from bad to worse and John Law fled the country. A decree of 10 October 1720 declared the notes of the bank no longer

32 The first assignats were interest-bearing, coloured, and showed the King

currency. The final winding up of the system involved the gathering of all the papers, notes, shares and other records and their official burning in a great public bonfire. It is for this reason that today collectors find these notes very scarce.

Seemingly the French were quick to forget this great financial disaster, for some 69 years later the revolutionary National Assembly—which had confiscated the property of the Church—showed a marked interest in the theory of land money. In 1789 John Law's treatise, 'Money and Trade Considered . . .,' was translated into French and put into force on a gigantic scale.

It might be as well to recall one or two of the main incidents of the revolution.

The first blood came on Monday 12 July 1789 when a procession followed a bust of the ejected minister Necker through Paris. Although the crowd was unarmed, Prince Lambesc's troops opened fire. A French guard chanced to be among those killed and thereupon the whole French guard sprang into revolt—

33 Citizen's note for 30 sols

the Parisian militia came into being and so did the famous tricolour of France—red, blue, the old colours of Paris, and white, signifying the groundwork of the new constitution. On 14 July the Bastille was stormed and subsequently levelled to the ground, symbolising the overthrow of the ancient and corrupt institutions of the monarchy.

The Jacobins emerged the stronger political power and Lafayette, who had made a name for himself in the American War of Independence against Britain, made the mistake of defying them. The Jacobins replied to Lafayette's manifesto by raising the Parisian populace against the National Assembly on 20 June 1792. They forced their way into the palace and there Louis XVI met them with admirable dignity—the King wore the Paris red cap, and the crowd was appeased—for a time.

But the court put their trust in foreign troops—the Duke of Brunswick had 80,000 men under his command and the Queen referring to this said: 'In a month I shall be free.' Frenchmen replied with violence and the vanguard was entrusted to the battalion of the men of Marseilles, who have attached their name to the ever famous-song, 'The Marseillaise.' The Swiss Guard at the palace was massacred.

The republic was formed and a new calendar born. 22 September 1792 became the first day of year 1 of the republic—and this form of dating soon appeared on the assignats. The abolition of royalty in France was proclaimed the day before. The new calendar came into force officially on 24 November.

ASSIGNATS

The proposal to issue assignats was made to the National Assembly on 19 September 1789 and this was for 500

The banknote depicts:

série 1956 · n.º 1407 · 50

République Française.
Assignat de cinquante LIVRES.
De la Création du 14. Décbre 1792.
Hypothéqué sur les ... l'An premier de la République, Domaines Nationaux.

LA LOI PUNIT DE MORT LE CONTREFACTEUR.

LA NATION RÉCOMPENSE LE DÉNONCIATEUR.

n.º 1407 · LIBERTÉ ÉGALITÉ · série 1956

34 50 livre assignat of 1792

million livres in notes bearing interest. These could be used to pay for the 'Patriotic Levy'—which was set at a quarter of a year's income per person. It will be remembered that patriotism was very high at this time and many people freely gave money and jewels to the government. In this climate such a levy was acceptable to the people.

The way was cleared for large issues of assignats when the revolutionaries confiscated the Church's lands and property. They did not put it quite like that, however. Maribeau delicately broke the news that the Church's property was to be 'at the disposition of the State' rather than 'belonging to the State', but it meant the same thing!

There were some men in France who were against the backing of money with land, but in the violent times of the revolution the proponents found no difficulty in silencing many of them for good. There was hardly any opposition when Baron de Çernon proposed the issue of assignats for 25, 50 and 100 livres which would not be interest-bearing like the earlier notes. Tallyrand's voice was one of the few heard in disapproval, stating that it would cause the disappearance of gold and silver.

A department was set up to issue the notes, 'the Caisse de l'Extraordinaire'. At first the National Assembly ordered property to be sold to a value equal to the notes—and the first issue of assignats was thus well secured. Further the notes were to be burnt on redemption. But government lands were valued as high as 3,000 million livres and this figure was 'written up' to 15 billion by 1793. The revolutionaries lost no time in issuing assignats to the limit! They did not sell the land to back them and

35 400 livres, with attractive vignette showing the cap of liberty. These notes were issued in 1792

36 Issued in Year 3 of the Republic this high denomination 10,000 franc note soon depreciated in value as inflation swept through the country

it was soon found that property was not selling. From a small discount the assignats fell to large discounts.

In 1792 things took a turn for the worse when France engaged in foreign war. The authorities, at the stroke of a pen, demonetised the 'Royal assignats' and thus saved themselves responsibility for over 1,000 million livres—using anti-monarchism as the pretext. But by November 1795 there were 20 billion livres in circulation. A decree was passed that no more assignats should be issued and on 19 February 1796 the printing plates were ceremoniously broken and

burned at the Place Vendôme before a large gathering of the people.

'Mandats territorials' were now issued in an attempt to redress the situation and old assignats were to be exchanged at the rate of 30 to 1 new mandat. Bearing in mind that in the months before destroying the assignat plates the government had virtually doubled the 20 billion notes in circulation, this meant there would be some 800 million mandats.

The mandats went the way of the assignats and ended with the general demonetisation of all paper money.

37, 38 The Mandat territorials followed the assignats and were intended to replace them. They lost value even more quickly than the assignats had done. The two illustrated are great rarities being handsigned on the reverse as examples for banks to compare against possible forgeries. Only 600 of each were issued as signed specimens

39 Billet de confiance 15 sols 1791

The treasury of France was empty and the government appealed for money to its soldiers who were then taking Italy by the sword. Nearly every despatch to the army was a begging letter for money—and to the surprise of all, the money came, far exceeding the expectations of the government. The man who sent the money was Napoleon Bonaparte and in a short time France was back on its feet and using gold and silver in normal business.

BILLETS DE CONFIANCE
Shortly before the French Revolution broke out many of the nobility had the foresight to leave the country, taking with them as much gold and silver as they could muster. This led to a situation where there was no small money in circulation and, as the first assignats of the revolution were for 50 livres, there was a great need for small money.

All over France towns and individuals issued their own notes in the form of *billets de confiance*, the first appearing at Montpellier in September 1790. These form an interesting field for the collector, as they come in all shapes and sizes, some printed, some written out. Between 1790 and 1793, 83 districts of France, involving some 1,500 towns and villages, issued nearly 6,000 different notes.

They were usually printed on paper but can be found on cardboard, parchment and on the backs of book plates. Great rarities among these are the French playing-card notes. Earlier, it will be remembered that French Canadians had used playing cards as money because of their durability—and today some of these Canadian playing cards fetch around $2,000. The French Revolution playing cards are not so well known, but nevertheless they are among the scarcest of the Revolution notes.

Today most of the *billets de confiance* are scarce because by an order of November 1792, which was enforced on 1 October 1793, all these notes were to be destroyed.

Pont du Chateau, a small village, was one of the few which did not comply with the order and consequently their notes are most frequently met with among collectors of these notes. Even so only 11,500 of the most common denomination, the 5 sous, were actually issued, and this, compared to stamp and coin issues, is very small indeed.

The largest number of different *billets de confiance* come from the department of Orne where 292 types are known; at the other extreme Landes issued only four types.

FORGERY

There is no question that the British Government sanctioned the forgery of French assignats, no doubt because it found the earlier results of forgery of American War of Independence notes very satisfactory to its purpose.

The British Government has never admitted these events, nor for that matter the forgery of German notes for propaganda purposes in World War II. But the evidence available for forgery of assignats is considerable.

While it is true that Hansard records do not show a debate in Parliament on the matter, in March 1794 the *Morning Chronicle*, *The Star*, *Lloyd's Evening Post*, the *London Chronicle* and other papers alluded to such a debate.

The *Morning Chronicle* wrote:

There was another circumstance which he [Sheridan] could not help mentioning, because it would be necessary for him to introduce a clause to prevent such scandalous abuse of the Revenue Laws. There was a mill for the manufacturing of paper to a great amount in this country, in which the forgery of French assignats was carried on. The Excise officer who attended this mill doubted whether he could suffer this sort of proceeding to pass, and, on making the necessary communications, he received what appears to him to be a sufficient authority for superintending this, as if it had been the regular and honest manufacture of paper, in the way of trade. He did not state this upon the loose hearsay; he could give the name of the mill if necessary. He thought it highly important, the Government to disavow, by its Ministers any share in such a scandalous proceeding.

The British Government remained ominously silent at this, the Chancellor of the Exchequer contenting himself with the remark: 'The information from those who commit forgery is not the best to rely upon'.

Louis Blanc, whose *History of the French Revolution* appeared in 1863, wrote that in fact Pitt had every reason to shuffle off the question. The evidence is only too clear from the correspondence and the confessions of Count Joseph de Puisaye, who was Pitt's confidential man of business in the British minister's dealings with the French royalists.

Puisaye set up in this country a mill for the purpose of forging assignats, and he publicly and most impudently boasted of the sinister power the fabrication of false assignats gave him against the French revolutionaries.

If further evidence is needed there is the legal action brought by Strongitharm against Lukyn for payment for engraving copper-plates upon which French assignats were to be forged. The defence was the immorality of the transaction. Strongitharm had, in the first instance, declined the business, but had undertaken it on being assured, by the agent of the defendant, that it was sanctioned by the government and was intended for the use of the Duke of York's army—then

41 'Good-for 1 sou'. Probably the smallest note ever issued

42 Pictorial billet de confiance

43, 44, 45 Playing card notes of the French Revolution. Playing cards were first used as money at the turn of the seventeenth century in French Canada. They were very successful and the French revolutionaries used similar notes in several towns

in Holland. The judgement was reported as follows:

Lord Kenyon [Chief Justice] said that if the present transaction was grounded on a fraud, or contrary to the laws of nations, he should have held the notes [given for payment] to be void; but that it did not appear that there was any fraud in the case, or any violation of positive law. Whether the issuing of these assignats for the purpose of distressing the enemy was lawful in carrying on the war he was not prepared to say. It was not in evidence that the plaintiff was a party to any fraud, or that it was ever communicated to him that the assignats were to be used for any improper purpose. On the contrary he supposed that they were circulated by the authority of the higher powers of the country, and therefore did not question the propriety or legality of the measure.

4: Siege Notes

MAFEKING

Few notes have such close association with historical events as do the bank-notes issued during the siege of Mafeking (1899-1900) under the authority of Brevet Colonel Robert S.S. Baden Powell—later to be Lord Baden Powell and founder of the Scout movement.

The £1 note, in particular, reflects the siege as it depicts the famous home-made gun 'The Wolf', nicknamed after Baden Powell who was known to the natives as 'The Wolf that never sleeps'. The siege lasted 217 days and 273 of the small garrison were killed, wounded or captured during that time.

Everything was in short supply—there was so little food that it was a hanging offence to steal even a sausage. Just how hungry everyone was can be gathered from the telegraph sent by Lady Sarah Wilson early in May: 'Breakfast consists of horse sausages; lunch, minced mule and curried locusts'.

A lucky find of 200 5 lb shells left over from the Jameson Raid resulted in the making of 'The Wolf' to fire them. An old iron steam pipe and a water tank lined with fire-bricks were used, while ingenuity at the railway foundry produced brass castings, the breech block, trunnion and rings. Baden Powell sketched the gun for the design of the £1 note together with a Union Jack, soldiers, and a woman and child.

The completed drawing was mounted, photographed and then printed by Mr E. C. Ross on ordinary notepaper by Ferro Prussiate process. It is believed that 683 notes were issued, produced at the rate of 20 per day. Each was hand signed by Mr R. Urry of the Standard Bank of South Africa and Captain H. Greener, the Chief Paymaster.

But the first design for the £1 note had been a drawing by Baden Powell

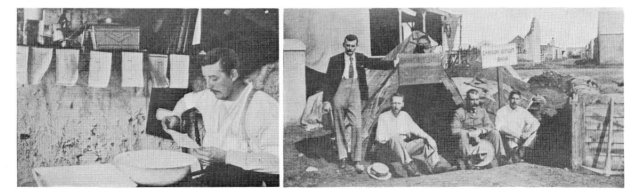

No. 638   No. 638

MAFEKING SIEGE NOTE
March 1900
ONE POUND
£1   £1

ISSUED BY AUTHORITY OF COLONEL R.S.S. BADEN POWELL.
(Commanding Rhodesian Forces)

This note is good for One Pound during the siege and will be exchanged for coin at the Standard Bank, Mafeking, on the resumption of Civil Law.

ENTERED   CHIEF PAYMASTER

47, 48 The production of siege notes was a very slow business — about six £1 notes an hour. On more than one occasion the bank was under fire from Boer forces. The Standard Bank of South Africa maintained the siege branch throughout the hostilities

of a soldier with a field gun and another soldier with a Maxim gun. The drawing, on copper, was etched out with acid, but problems arose. Baden Powell himself recorded them: 'We tried various dodges, drew a design on copper, bit it out with acid all right, but could not get sufficient pressure to print it though we tried it through a mangle, then we cut a croquet mallet in half and made a wood cut'.

Mr C. Riesle, the local watchmaker, engraved the woodcut but although one or two trial printings for the £1 note were produced from it the impression was not good enough. However, it was later modified to serve as the design for the 10 shilling notes.

The 10 shilling notes were first printed in March 1900 and the printed line at the bottom of the note: 'Issued

by authority of Col R. S. S. Baden-Powell, commanding frontier forces' contained an error, 'Commanding' being spelt 'Commaning' without the 'd'. Well over 1,000 were printed before the mistake was noticed and the error was corrected on subsequent printings.

Low value notes were printed on white 'Croxley' writing paper in blue ink, with the values of the notes in a different colour—1s green, 2s brown, 3s red. The 3s note is almost as rare as the £1 note as there was only one issue.

The stock of notes was kept in an underground office under the control of Captain Greener and Sergeant Major Jollie. In this office the Bechuanaland Protectorate embossed stamp was applied and the serial numbers and signatures added. The *Mafeking Mail* of 7 March contains a report of the theft of some of these notes. A native, Jim Phuthego,

50 During a shortage of paper money at Bulawayo, cards were issued and used as money to the value of the stamps stuck to them

49

took £5 worth of uncompleted notes and tried to pass them in the town. Because they bore no signatures, nor the Bechuanaland stamp he was soon arrested. On being found guilty he was given twenty lashes and three months hard labour.

The numbers of all notes were entered in a special register kept by the Standard Bank of South Africa. It is known that 7,000 10 shilling notes were issued and £1,045 7s worth of the 1s, 2s, and 3s, notes. Most of the notes were kept as souvenirs—indeed so avid were souvenir hunters that even before the siege was over the *Mafeking Mail* carried advertisements selling the siege postage stamps!

The total face value of notes issued came to £5,228 7s, and by January 1908 only £638 had been presented for redemption leaving £4,590 presumably held by souvenir collectors of the siege.

Although not strictly paper money, the garrison also issued special soup and sowen tickets—and as far as the inhabitants were concerned these were as good as banknotes.

The siege came to an end on 17 May 1900 when forces under Colonel Plummer and Colonel Mahon entered the town at 6 pm. Among them was Baden Powell's brother, Major Baden Powell.

KHARTOUM

The story of General Gordon's heroic defence of Khartoum, his violent death at the hands of the dervishes and the sack of Khartoum are well known. As a military man he had discharged his duty well and warned his superiors of his untenable position. But the relief forces he required were, through lack of perception by officials, sent too late.

Not so well known is the story of the siege notes. These are highly prized among collectors because many of them contain the hand-written signature of General 'Chinese' Gordon, and the general was himself responsible for their redemption, an entry in his *Journal* reading:

I offered in paying the three months 'Backsheesh' to the troops, to give orders for bulk sums, £120, £130 but they refused to accept them, they want regular paper money, so I have issued £10,000 more in £50 notes. In this paper money I am personally responsible for the liquidation and anyone can bring action against me, in my individual capacity, to recover the money, while in the orders it might be a query whether they [authorities in Cairo] might not decline to pay the orders. Paper cannot be bought at a discount, people have tried to buy it up, but have failed.

When the dervishes put Khartoum to the sword niceties of civilisation such as organised currency and filing systems were lost in the bloodbath. Fortunately for students the Governor General of the Sudan, Sir John Maffey, began making inquiries in Cairo in 1930 about the siege notes, and persevered for over a year until the surviving notes were discovered. Ismail Pasha Sidby, the Prime Minister of Egypt, then sent the notes in March 1931 to the Governor General for the benefit of 'the Gordon Memorial Fund.' Sir John instructed his private secretary, Mr M. W. Parr, CBE (subsequently in 1936 a successor to General Gordon as governor of the equatorial province) to make a detailed examination of the notes themselves, and to gather information about them. With the valuable help of Mr Bill Tarttelin MBE and Sir Said Pasha Shoucair some of the story has been unearthed—twelve complete sets of notes were found to exist, some of which are now preserved in institutions connected with the memory of Gordon Pasha.

When Gordon arrived at Khartoum in February 1884 he found the treasury nearly empty and pay for troops and officials was already three months in arrears. Arrangements had been made for Gordon to draw £100,000 from the Egyptian Treasury. During transport, however, some £40,000 disappeared into the pockets of Arab officials and only £60,000 reached Berber. A high official of the Egyptian Government found some excuse for 'acquiring' it and was subsequently to be rewarded with decorations and a pension on his return to Egypt.

Gordon received nothing and had no alternative but to issue paper money. Had

52 General Gordon personally signed many of the Khartoum siege notes

53

54, 55 100 piastre Khartoum note (right) and (below) another design note. There were many different types in circulation — some contemporary forgeries

he not done so the brave little garrison would not have been able to hold out for so long against the large Arab army under the Mahdi.

Notes were issued dated 25 April 1884. For a long time there was doubt about who designed the notes. Atabani said that Gordon designed them. Matbaghi said his brother Hassan Bey Ibrahim Matbaghi, head of the printing press, did so.

We know too from the *Journal* that up to 15 December Gordon had issued notes to the value of Egyptian £78,000 and that of this figure £18,000 was in the government treasury and £60,000 in circulation. Further sums were issued and Mr Parr's extensive research suggests £E168,500 as being the probable total. Pay rates were high—Gordon trebled workmen's pay to stop them deserting to the Mahdi, and compensation had to be paid to owners of buildings destroyed for military reasons. The Governor of Sennar received £15,000 worth of notes, and the whole of this amount was destroyed by the dervishes during the sack of the town. Many notes were publicly burned, thrown into the streets to be eaten by goats, and so on. To be caught in possession of Gordon notes meant a brutal death penalty.

But some notes were hidden and gradually, at the risk of their owners' lives, they made the terrible journey across the desert, hidden in clothing or at the bottom of grain bags until they reached Egypt. In Egypt some were honoured and many more were repudiated. Mr Parr records: 'After ignominious law-suits and bickerings they passed into oblivion so completely that they escaped the order for their own destruction, and it took over a year's search to find them!'

At Khartoum Mr Parr examined each note individually and produced the following tables:

Value	Numbers Examined	Lowest Serial No	Highest Serial No	Estimated Total Issue	Total Value £E
5 PT	39	72	16545	20,000	1,000
10 PT	184	302	14249	15,000	1,500
20 PT	423	310	26104	30,000	6,000
100 PT	1,215	915	19948	20,000	20,000
500 PT	226	13	2000	2,000	10,000
1000 PT	99	15	991	1,000	10,000
2000 PT	54	29	498	500	10,000
2500 PT	1,041	27	1980	2,000	50,000
5000 PT	193	202	1178	1,000	50,000
£E 50	12	12	178	200	10,000
				91,700	£E168,500

There is much confusion over the number of different denominations used. For instance, Ibrahim Ali Matbaghi, who worked in Gordon's press, claimed they were values of £100, £200, and £500. Naum Pasha Shoucair, in his history of the Sudan, refers to notes of values between 5 and 10pt and notes of 30 and 50pt, but none has come to light. Mr Parr carried on an extensive correspondence to ascertain the truth and a letter from Said Pasha Shoucair states: 'The fact that there are no notes of Pt 30 or Pt 50 in the Gordon College Museum, where the set is believed to be complete, nor at the Caisse de le Dette amongst the notes presented for repayment, seems to lead to the inference that none existed and that Naum was misinformed.'

It is now believed that the full issues comprise 1, 5, 10 and 20pt, £1, 5, 10, 20, 25, 50 and 5,000pt.

All these notes can be found with two types of signatures, manuscript and hectograph. It seems that Gordon hand-signed some 50,000 notes. Clearly this toil was too great and the head of the press was directed to find some alternative method. The immense variety of hectograph signatures demonstrates that many were experimental, and the worn remains on existing notes show that generally they were unsatisfactory.

But the examination of existing notes gives the collector an idea of the stage at which notes were hectographed instead of hand-signed.

Denomination	Change from MS to Hectograph takes place between		Total Issue
5 PT	15,000 and	16,217	20,000
10 PT	8,476 and	8,754	15,000
20 PT	10,820 and	10,991	30,000
£5	552 and	583	2,000
£10	469 and	510	1,000
£20	159 and	165	500

In the case of the £1 notes there is no clear-cut dividing line. Up to 11,962 they were signed in manuscript and then to 15,976 in hectograph. From number 15,982 they were manuscript again. One can infer that Gordon decided the hectograph signature was not satisfactory—or was not so readily received by the populace.

It is known that some 3,500 notes existed in 1931 for Mr Parr himself examined them!; but he does not know where they are now.

The dervishes in Khartoum learned that notes had been smuggled to Egypt and cashed. They realised they had been destroying good money! Streets were dug up where notes had been scattered and notes were smuggled out of Egypt. It is known that even the Khalifa's camel-postman helped to smuggle notes into Egypt.

When the official supply dried up notes were forged. Fortunately for collectors these are easy to detect. The seal was forged and the writing was different from the other notes; the lithographed signature was copied from one of the hasty manuscript signatures and not written with the care Gordon gave to all the other lithographed signatures. The number of the note and the seal were lithographed instead of added later as in the case of all other notes, and in place of 'Nigri' there was written 'Yigri'.

Naturally, the authorities were not keen to redeem Khartoum notes at a time when the Mahdi was in control of Khartoum and even after British soldiers marched in they had no true knowledge of the issues made by General Gordon— and they knew there were forgeries about! But Mr Parr has now set the record as straight as it can ever be.

COLBERG

The small, handsigned notes of Colberg issued during the siege of 1807 give testimony to the stubborn defence of the fortified seaport town of Prussia. Colberg

56 Colberg siege note dated 1807. The notes were completely hand-written

was surrounded by some 18,000 troops under the commands of Feulie, Loison and Mortier, but despite this the town managed to keep a force of 'free-fighters' outside the city walls under Schill while the town burgher, Nettelbeck, maintained the city defences from within. Together they succeeded in defending the town until the Peace of Tilsit brought the war to a close.

It was not the first time Colberg had been under siege. In the Thirty Years War it was captured by the Swedes after a long siege in 1631, and in the Seven Years War it was one of the major centres of conflict. In 1758 it withstood the attacks of General Palmbach and in 1760 it held out against the Russian and Swedish forces, both by sea and land, until Werner came to the town's relief. The following year, however, it was forced to surrender to Romanzoff after a four-month siege.

MAINZ (in French, Mayence)

Mainz is one of the oldest cities in Germany. Its strategic importance was recognised by the Romans who, under Drusus, in 13 BC erected a fortified camp there. On three occasions it was almost totally destroyed, by the Alemanni, the Vandals and the Huns (451 AD). Gutenberg invented printing at Mainz in 1440.

In 1792 the citizens of Mainz welcomed the principles of the French Revolution. The park, Neue Anlage, is laid on the site of the Chateau de Favorite, where the Duke of Brunswick signed his famous manifesto to the French people in 1792. The gates of the city were opened to the French Republican troops under General Custine. The Prussian army immediately laid siege to the city and after much hardship the city was forced to surrender the

57 *This siege note of Mainz was made on the reverse of an ordinary 10 assignat note of the French Revolution dated 1791. The siege date is 1793*

following year. However, it was ceded to France by the Peace of Campo Formio in 1797 and was not restored to Germany until 1814.

During the siege French assignats were often overprinted for use as siege money and towards the close of 1793 special siege notes were issued.

VENICE and Italian Independence

A set of four notes recalls the grim struggle for Italian freedom in 1848-9 and, because the rising was crushed, these notes remain the most common of all siege notes.

They tell a sad story. Napoleon Buonaparte, much maligned in British history books, was the first to see that the Italians were ready for self-government and his government of Italy was liberal and enlightened. Italy has never forgotten this debt to Napoleon but the foundations he laid were destroyed with his defeat at Waterloo. The Treaty of Vienna set out to reverse everything he had attempted to do and Italy was

returned to its old rulers. For the next thirty years attempts to restore the freedoms introduced by Napoleon were ruthlessly cut down by Austrian arms. In 1832 Giuseppe Mazzini, a Genoese, had founded the famous secret society of Young Italy. It was supported by the free-thinkers and writers of the day and soon became a power to reckon with.

At the beginning of 1848 the rising began. Sicily took up arms against the rule of Naples and Naples in its turn against the king. Austria proclaimed martial law in her Italian domains but Milan refused to submit and during her Five Glorious Days, starting on 18 March, bravely resisted superior forces.

Venice went further and it declared itself a republic. Because of its natural defences the people of Venice were able to withstand the powerful forces which immediately laid siege to the city. Throughout the year battles raged but gradually the Austrian forces got the upper hand, and when Charles Albert

suffered the disastrous defeat of Novara, Venice was the only place of importance that still held out. The besieged, led by Daniel Manin, held out until their resources were completely exhausted. The women of Venice even turned their jewellery into money. Finally, decimated by famine and pestilence, Venice surrendered under treaty.

In 1850 the tyrants returned. But

one man had not given up the struggle. The founder of Young Italy, Giuseppe Mazzini, had proclaimed the Republic of Rome in 1848 and served on the triumvirate of the new state. With the defeat of the Roman Army by French forces and those of other nations, Mazzini was forced into exile. Mazzini (1805-72) was a republican and patriot closely identified with Garibaldi's movement. He had sown the seed of Italian unity and in exile continued his struggle. He produced notes for the National Italian Loan of 1850 intending to raise 10 million lire 'directed solely to speed up the independence and liberty of Italy'.

Five values were printed ranging from 1 Franco to 100 Franchi and all had the inscriptions 'God and the People' beneath a trumpet, and 'Italy and Rome' under a sabre. The ancient symbols of Roman authority, the Fasces, form part of the design together with seals of the republic and the committee. The military nature of the notes was emphasised by stacked muskets, drum and cannon balls.

These notes (*Prestito Nazionale Italiano*) were very successful because of the patriotic feeling of the people, and Mazzini lived to see Italian unity. In October 1860 Garibaldi arrived in time to turn defeat into victory at Volturno. He met Victor Emmanuel at Teano, hailed him King of Italy and handed over his conquests to him. Rome remained under the French for another decade until their defeat at Sedan left the Italians free to enter the city under arms on 20 September 1871. The following year Rome became the capital and the unity of Italy was complete.

60 The Mazzini note issued to raise funds to carry on the war for Italian independence

5: Africa and the Middle East

Africa is still a mysterious continent, great parts of which remain among the unmapped primitive areas of the world. It covers one fifth of the world's land surface and is inhabited by over 250 million people who speak more than a thousand different languages.

Only ten years ago less than one third of the African population, who lived in an area not exceeding 10 per cent of the continent, were independent. Now, in 1972, ninety African nations have gained

61 Moise Tshombe, who declared Katanga an independent republic. The new nation did not last long and these banknotes are almost the only mementoes of Katanga available

independence and are spread over 85 per cent of the area. These facts influence the currency and monetary systems no less than they do other political and economic factors. In 1966 alone Tanzania, Kenya and Uganda put new banknote issues into circulation.

CONGO-KATANGA

The Congo gained independence from what was formerly the Belgian Congo in 1960. King Boudouin handed over authority to the newly elected leader, Joseph Kasavabu on 30 June as a result of the earlier Round Table conference which had taken place in Brussels. Simultaneously, Patric Lumumba was elected president of the new state.

The country was very soon in political trouble. The president of the Federation of the Katangan Associations, Moise Tshombe, declared Katanga to be an independent state with himself as the head of the new nation. Patrice Lumumba, meanwhile, was overthrown by Col Mobutu who took over control of the state at the head of the army.

Moise Tshombe established Elizabeth-ville as the capital of Katanga and almost immediately issued currency notes. His portrait appeared on these notes which were dated '31.10.60'. The currency, of course, was considered to be illegal by the Mobutu government, as was the 'independent state' itself. By the time the Kinshasa forces reached Elizabethville, Tshombe had escaped and obtained political asylum in Spain. He was tried in his absence at a military court headed by Mobutu and his issue of 'illegal' currency was among the counts against him. He was sentenced to death.

In a dramatic air hijacking, he fell into the hands of Mobutu's agents. Although he was not immediately executed, he died a few years later in an Algerian prison under circumstances that have still to be clarified.

BIAFRA

On 30 May 1967 Lt Col Ojukwu announced that the eastern region of Nigeria would form a new republic, to be named Biafra. Almost immediately the Federal Military Government of Nigeria under Lt Col Gowan ordered

62 Colonel Mobutu, President of the Congo, who overthrew Patrice Lumumba and headed the military court which was to sentence Tshombe to death

63 Biafra, the breakaway state of Eastern Nigeria, was involved in some of the most horrifying warfare and starvation of the last quarter-century. Biafra issued several denominations of paper money during its fight for survival

general mobilisation, imposing strict sanctions on the breakaway state.

British families were advised to evacuate the area and blockades were formed to prevent Biafra from exporting her crude oil, the main source of income on which the new state intended to base its economy. By mid-July the Federal Government in Lagos had launched several attacks on the self-proclaimed republic, but the Ibo tribes, who formed the population of Biafra, successfully resisted and soon joined forces with mutinous soldiers of the Nigerian army.

Soon after announcing its secession from the rest of Nigeria, the newly proclaimed independent Republic of Biafra made arrangements for its own paper money to be printed in Portugal and Switzerland. Surplus quantities of this paper money survived the short-lived state.

At first the Biafran currency was at par with the pound sterling. Inflation, however, soon began to take a grip on the war economy and reached such proportions that a packet of cigarettes cost in the region of £1 sterling and a single egg was priced at £2!

The war was to continue for almost three years, causing great concern among the civilised nations of the world, until the Biafrans were gradually starved into surrender.

By the time Biafra capitulated (9 January 1970) tens of thousands had met death through starvation and many more from both sides had been killed in bloody battles. Biafra was to be wiped off the map.

Geneva agents of the Bank of Biafra sold publicly large quantities of their banknotes in all denominations from 5s to £5. Some of these notes are extremely difficult to obtain owing to the small quantity that were printed.

GERMAN EAST AFRICA

When Dr Karl Peters, the founder of the Society for German colonisation, travelled to Zanzibar in 1884, the island was ruled by a sultanate that had been recognised by the British as early as 1862. But Dr Peters was able to persuade native chiefs on the mainland to accept the protection of the German Kaiser. These arrangements were recognised by the German Government in February

1885 and German East Africa was run by a company of that name. It was only after fierce opposition by local tribes and many bloody battles that the German East Africa Company's rule and responsibility were removed and Imperial administration was established.

Britain's involvement in these early stages of the German colony was quite limited, although she was instrumental in the defeat that the Germans were to suffer in that area three decades later. In spite of meek objections in support of Zanzibar's sultan, the British Government soon acquiesced and instructions were forwarded to the British consul in Zanzibar to co-operate with the Germans. By an agreement concluded in London between Great Britain, France and Germany in 1886, Germany was granted all rights in the territory. Opposition from Arabs and African tribes was fierce and continued until 1907, when the bloodiest of the battles known as the 'Maji-Maji rising' was suppressed. After that the country settled down and began to develop economically.

Coinage was widely used and the only paper money was promissory and credit notes used by the local people, who accepted them as legal tender. In 1905 the German East Africa Bank was established in Dar es Salaam. Notes of 5, 10, 50 and 100 rupees, printed in Germany, were issued. In 1912 a 500 rupee note was also issued.

The most interesting currency issued by the Germans in East Africa were

64 The young Kaiser shown on the German East Africa notes of 1905

notes which were considered to be provisional by the Germans as they did not expect the world war to continue for a great length of time. These 'interim notes' were issued in March 1915 and printed, rather crudely, in different sizes and on different coloured coarse paper in Dar es Salaam and Tobora. Two years later, just before the German defeat, an issue of these interim notes appeared which have since become known as 'bush notes'. These, which were even more primitive than the earlier

issues, were printed by means of a children's rubber printing set during the German retreat through the bush.

German East Africa was occupied by British and Belgian troops after Germany's defeat. By the Treaty of Versailles Germany gave up her sovereignity over the territory which became a British and Belgian mandate. The former colony of German East Africa is now Tanzania.

TURKEY

During its five-hundred-year span from the fifteenth century to World War I, the Ottoman Empire encompassed large territories of Europe, the Middle East and Africa. Historians claim that the character of the empire throughout its existence assured the final downfall of the sultanate. This came soon after World War I and Kemal Ataturk's declaration of the Democratic Republic of Turkey in 1923 marked the end of the Turkish Empire and the beginning of a new era of modernisation and democracy.

Many countries under Ottoman rule had their own money and their currencies circulated in other parts of the empire. The earliest paper currency of the Turks was issued by Sultan Abdul Mejid who ruled from 1839 to 1861. It was issued in 1848 and circulated within a limited area of the empire.

Early issues were also put into circulation by Abdul-Aziz, but were replaced by Turkish treasury notes known as the 'Kaime' in July 1876. The areas into which these notes were introduced, mainly the Middle East, had not used paper money before and they were issued for the payment of taxes. In fact, 'Kaime' notes were not legally valid for any other purpose and were not exchangeable for coins. Though the notes

did circulate among the people they quickly lost value as they were unconvertible.

The most interesting notes issued by the Ottomans were those put into circulation under Abdul Reshat V. These very colourful notes, in denominations from one gurush (100 gurush = one livre) to 50,000 livres, were put into circulation in some African and Asian countries during World War II. Printed in Germany, Austria and England, they were backed by loans that Turkey obtained from Germany and Austria-Hungary at the outbreak of World War I. The first of these notes was issued on 30 March 1915 by the Turkish Ministry of Finance. A clause on all the notes states that they are redeemable in gold. Arabic script was used for the Turkish text on the notes. Although they ceased to circulate in 1920 they were still being redeemed by the Turkish government as late as 1948.

GALLIPOLI OVERPRINT

Turkish notes issued during World War I are sometimes referred to as the Dardenelles issue, because they circulated in Turkey when the British and French naval bombardment of Gallipoli Peninsula took place in February 1915. On 7 March of that year some 120,000 Englishmen, Frenchmen, Australians, New Zealanders and Ghurkas under the command of General Sir Ian Hamilton

67 (left) Kaime notes of 1876 were not legal tender but the local people used them as legal tender until they began to lose value

68 (right) Only from the reverse of the note can one tell the date of issue of the 'Kaimes'. The Muslim date appears within the circular stamp at the top and the French name of the bank, place of issue and Gregorian date appear at the bottom

69 *An Ottoman £5 note redeemable in gold*

70 *Kemal Ataturk whose declaration of the Democratic Republic of Turkey in 1923 finally ended the old Turkish Empire*

were landed in Gallipoli. This landing has been regarded as one of the most badly organised campaigns in British military history. The object of easing the burden on the Western Front and reaching Constantinople failed completely. Only later did General Allenby successfully defeat the Turks and bring about the collapse of the empire.

Many collectors of British and Palestinian banknotes proudly display the famous 'Gallipoli overprint' notes in their collections. These were the second treasury issue by the British Government which were given to troops for use in the Dardenelles and for such purpose the denominations were overprinted in Turkish. Only 10s and £1 notes were issued and the latter is a great rarity.

A great deal of research has been done to resolve the confusion over the exact circumstances under which these notes were issued. It is, however, now accepted that the notes circulated in Egypt and Palestine as well as Turkey during and after the campaign. The notes without the overprint were made legal tender in Malta to facilitate soldiers on leave from the Turkish front.

ISRAEL

Situated at the crossroads of four continents, Israel's history is steeped in Jewish, Christian and Islamic tradition.

The state was established in 1948 after 2,000 years of Jewish exile in the Diaspora, and important historical events took place in the months preceeding and following the creation of the new state on 15 May.

On that day the British, who had a mandatory status over Israel given to them by the League of Nations in 1920, left Palestine in a state of administrative chaos.

The country was under threat of invasion by several Arab states. The economic situation could have led to disaster but for the initiative and pre-cautionary measures taken by the well-established Anglo Palestine Bank and the provisional government of the state.

At the beginning of 1948 it became apparent that the British mandate over Palestine would very soon cease. In the knowledge that the British would have little concern in ensuring the organised transfer of the currency system, the bank, under the auspices of the Jewish National Authorities, began to hoard Palestine Currency Board notes. These were on a par with the pound sterling (and are still redeemable by the Crown Agents in pounds sterling at face value).

A month later Palestine was dropped from the sterling area and its sterling holdings in London were blocked.

The manager of the Anglo Palestine Bank, Mr E. L. Hoffien, had in the meantime travelled to the USA to negotiate with the American Banknote

71 The 'Gallipoli' overprint. British treasury notes were overprinted in Turkish. This note, '60 Gumus Kurus' loosely translated means 'Sixty silver piastres'

Company the printing of currency for the new state of Israel. Simultaneously, other officers of the bank had local money printed although this was illegal under the British administration. The notes were kept for an emergency, but were completely destroyed without ever being issued.

Mr Hoffien met far greater problems than he had expected. To negotiate on behalf of a country that was not a sovereign state was not easy. A monetary unit had not been decided upon, nor was an issuing institute established. Finally, the time factor was impossible to co-ordinate: Israel needed the notes badly and the American Banknote Company was unable to do the job in less than 18 months.

Somehow all of these problems were solved but they shrank in importance beside the problem of delivery. The only Israeli airport, Lod, was in Arab hands and no Israeli transport planes were avilable. Consequently the notes were delivered by the Royal Dutch Airlines to a temporary airfield in the north of Israel. From there they were transported by armoured car to Haifa and finally to the banks' vaults in Tel Aviv, where they arrived in July 1948.

The notes were the first official issues of the government of Israel and were put into circulation on 18 August 1948, the day after the passing of the Bank Note Ordinance Act by the Israeli Parliament. This ordinance authorised the Anglo Palestine Bank to become the note-issuing body of the country and separately decreed the new Israel pound to replace the Palestine pound. The notes that had been issued, and were now official legal tender of the sovereign state of Israel, became a peculiarity, although this escaped the eyes of the ordinary people: the denomination on the notes stated Palestine pounds while the official currency was, of course, the Israel pound. The legal tender clause was only later overprinted on the note, while the meaningless words 'The bank will accept this note for payment in any account' appeared on the face. Furthermore, probably for the first time in history, this currency was backed by another country's paper money, the Palestine Currency Board notes of Britain!

With time the whole military and economic situation came under control and the Anglo Palestine Bank was replaced by the Bank Leumi Le-Israel in 1952. The new notes, also printed by the American Banknote Company (who refused to place the name of the firm on the notes owing to the low-quality printing caused by the hurried delivery of the notes), were identical but for the new heading and denomination, which was now in Israel pounds.

72 The Palestine Currency Board. A British controlled note-issuing authority. While very rare, they would still be redeemed at face by the Crown Agents

73 The Anglo Palestine Bank Limited £5

6: The Making of Latin America

The American sub-continent has rarely been involved in world conflicts and its major contact with the rest of the world was during the Spanish and Portuguese colonial period. Internal strife and struggle, however, have been frequent and often bloody, with revolutions, counter-revolutions, and disputes with neighbouring nations. Periods of unrest have a telling influence on the economy of a country and a great deal of Latin America's history of war and conflict can be told through the paper currency of the times.

MEXICO

Two names stand out in Latin American history which rank with that of Robin Hood in English legend. Both were deeply involved in the Mexican Revolution at the beginning of the twentieth century and led eventful and colourful lives, the consequences of which were of great importance to Mexico's future development. Both issued their own 'banknotes'.

The two men were the revolutionary patriots Francisco 'Pancho' Villa and Emiliano Zapata. They were instrumental in the movement which finally led Mexico to restore to peasant villagers their rights of participation in government and national development.

The Mexican Revolution took place because the politicians failed to agree as to who would succeed the elderly dictatorial president, Porfirio Diaz; Francisco Madero started the revolution in 1910, but three years after the downfall of President Diaz, Madero was assassinated and Mexico was once more under a ruthless dictator—Victoriano Huerta. Huerta was ousted by Venusiano Carranza who was finally overthrown in 1920 by his own lieutenant, Obregon. This new president was to lead Mexico out of the revolution into a period of relative peace and prosperity.

Born Doroteo Arango in Rio Grande, Northern Mexico, on 4 October 1877, 'Pancho' Villa spent his early years as a bandit chief, becoming sufficiently notorious by the age of thirty to have a price put on his head by Porfirio Diaz. He was very willing, therefore, to join Madero in the revolt against Diaz.

Emiliano Zapata's background is more impressive. He was born in Anencuilco in the southern state of Morelos about 1870. The Zapata family was famous in the area. Their name was made during the war of independence (1810-20) when Emiliano's grandfather, as a boy, delivered food and ammunition to the Mexican insurgents fighting against the Spaniards. Two of his father's brothers had fought in the War of Reform and against the French invasion in the 1860s; and Jose Zapata, whose exact relationship to Emiliano is not clear, had long established himself as a hero and almost mythical leader of the people of Anencuilco. It was with such a personal background that Emiliano Zapata was elected president of the village council in August 1909.

He became the leader of the southern revolutionaries who swore their allegiance to Madero, as Pancho Villa had done in the north. Zapata patiently bid for Madero's favour, confident that this new leader would do justice to the villagers. He was badly let down. The influence of the planters induced the weak Madero to break his revolutionary promises. Zapata negotiated with the Federalists for the return of lands to their true owners, avoiding bloodshed for as long as possible, but all to no avail. Madero was murdered and Zapata, like Villa, had a new enemy in Huerta.

Pancho Villa had escaped to Texas when Madero was murdered but now, hearing of the new revolutionary movement under Carranza, he returned to form the constitutionalist movement. The aim and ambition of this group was the destruction of Huerta. Villa met with success after success. Among his victories was the taking of Chihuahua and on 8 December 1913 Pancho Villa was appointed temporary governor of the city.

Within a few days, having received Carranza's consent, Villa issued paper currency in eleven denominations, all headed 'Tesoreria General del Estado de Chihuahua' and bearing his title and full

74 The smallest of the 'Sabanas de Villa' is this 25 centavos note on which Villa's name appears in full. The denominations increased in size in relation to value. Other issues by Villa were printed by the American Bank-note Company and were put into circulation without signatures as no bank was yet in existence to issue the notes

name as General Francisco Villa. These notes, the size of which increased in relation to the denominations, were referred to as 'Las Sabanas de Villa' meaning 'Villa's sheets'.

Although these are the only issues bearing his name, Pancho Villa was responsible for several more issues, including 10 million pesos worth of Banco del Estado de Chihuahua dated 12 December 1913, which were printed by the American Banknote Company. Some other notes were known as 'Dos Caritas' because of the two portraits appearing on them, one of which was of

Madero. Villa also revalidated, in 1914, the paper money which had originally been issued by the provisional government of Carranza.

A militarist rather than an economist, Villa could see no way to cover the increasing expenses of his campaign other than by issuing additional currency. It is ironical that he himself should have been angered by the high cost of living in the areas in which his money circulated and which had been caused by his own inflationary measures.

Zapata and Villa now decided to form a coalition in order to consolidate the revolutionary forces and form a strong front. They met in Mexico City and widely advertised their intentions which, however, were doomed to failure.

The stronger of the two, Pancho Villa, believed in a constitutionalist approach which, in principle, contradicted Zapata's 'plan of Ayala'. The latter was based on an agrarian reform which would lead to the emancipation of the poorer classes and equality in land ownership. Although Zapata's theories were to become the foundation of Mexico's agricultural development, Pancho Villa was considered the bigger thorn in the Government's side. Discord between the two revolutionaries facilitated Carranza's recapture of Mexico City and his forces directed all their attention towards Pancho Villa and the north.

It was in this period of temporary peace in the south, that the 'Zapatistas' organised themselves into a tidy and select society. They elected provisional authorities and a 'public security force' was set up. Although Zapata's interference with the administration was limited, it would seem that it is during this period that he was responsible for issuing currency. This was in late autumn 1914.

The southern and central states of Mexico which had been under Zapata's control had already been flooded with currency printed on cardboard from different sources, some of which was intended to finance Zapatista forces. Inevitably such irresponsible issues soon lost public confidence and so the fictitious 'Banco Revolucionario de Guerrero' was formed. Guerrero was the largest and most densely populated state of southern Mexico, in close proximity to Morelos. The capital, Ghilpancingo, was a prestigious city and its name appears on all the banknotes. They were dated 6 October, 20 October, 1 November and 1 December 1914 and the denominations were for 1, 2, 5, 10 and 20 pesos. It is possible that the intention was for Zapata's men actually to establish such a bank, and that this intention was frustrated by the resumption of fighting. Whatever the case may have been, the 'banknotes' circulated as currency in spite of the fact that the bank was non-existent and its creation was one-man's decision—without any kind of backing, financial or legal.

When Carranza's forces recaptured Mexico City and he was reinstated as President, the new government was almost immediately recognised by the United States.

Pancho Villa expressed his anger by crossing the border and, with 400 men, attacked Columbus in southern USA, killing several citizens and partly burning the city.

Carranza, rather surprisingly, refused to allow US troops to pursue Pancho Villa who remained under arms for several years. His retirement was finally bought by the Federals in 1920 when a land grant brought an end to his unscrupulous activities.

By this time Zapata had been sadly betrayed by Carranza. Promising to meet him in order to negotiate a settlement, Zapata was invited in April of the

76 'Banco Revolucionario de Guerrero' never existed in spite of the comparative high quality of the banknotes. This issue of Zapata's notes enjoyed a considerable circulation

same year to attend a conference. He did not hesitate to accept; little did he know of the treachery that lay ahead. In the words of an eyewitness:

. . . having formed ranks, [Carranza's] guards looked ready to do him the honours. Three times the bugle sounded the honour call, and as the last note died away, as the General in Chief [Zapata] reached the threshold of the door . . . at point blank range, without giving him time to even draw his pistols, the soldiers who were presenting arms fired two volleys, and our unforgettable General Zapata fell never to rise again . . .

Carranza was overthrown by Obregon a few months after Zapata's death and by the time Pancho Villa was mysteriously assassinated in 1923, Mexico was well out of the revolution and on the way to recovery. However, over the next few years Obregon's rule realised many of the ambitions of the revolutionary movement.

CUBA

Cuba is the second largest island in the Atlantic, (Great Britain being the largest) and although it was the first land in the New World to be discovered by Columbus, in 1492, it was the last to be freed from Spanish occupation (1898). Independence came after the 1895 revolt led by Jose Marti—the heroic poet and revolutionary whose portrait appears on many Cuban notes.

Cuba's modern history has been relatively free of revolts, but because of her close proximity to the USA there was serious concern in the western hemisphere when Castro officially proclaimed Cuba a communist state on 1 May 1961.

A former Army Sergeant, Fulgencio Batista had been a leading figure in Cuban politics during the 1930s and in 1940 he was elected president. However, one year after Batista's proclamation of a dictatorship, Dr Fidel Castro Ruz formed a revolutionary movement. The guerilla activities of the cigar smoking, bearded revolutionaries are well known. This movement gained gradual momentum and on the 1 January 1959 Castro and his followers triumphantly marched into Havana, having caused Batista to flee the island. This revolutionary scene and many others are shown on the modern banknotes of Cuba.

Castro's first actions upon gaining power were the suspension of the constitution, the election of a ruling 'junta'

77(a) Castro's 'Declaration of Havana', 2 September 1960

72

and a brief trip to Washington, where he was unable to obtain support for his movement. The USA broke diplomatic relations with Cuba in 1961—as did other countries outside the Communist block.

One particular 'coup', however, was overshadowed by other events which threatened a third world war. This was the decree issued on 5 August 1961—a Saturday—cancelling the validity of all circulating notes on Monday 7 August! Castro's official excuse for this drastic step was that it was designed to put an end to the illegal flow of currency into Cuba. Refugees had fled when he assumed power and had taken millions of Cuban pesos with them. The interpretation given by American officials was that the decree proved Castro was in economic trouble. In any case, a complete set of new Cuban banknotes were issued.

Possibly the most interesting of these is the first series of the 1961 issue where Ernesto Guevara's signature appears. This Argentinian, who at one time was second to Castro among the revolutionary leaders, was made President of the National Bank in 1960. Very much in line with his independent character, the notes were signed 'Che'—his nickname! These are the only known national bank notes on which the signatory has used only his christian name.

COLOMBIA

Modern Colombia underwent several major upheavals before achieving relative peace at the beginning of this century. In the nineteenth century alone the country was torn apart by no less than forty revolutions and ten civil wars culminating in the 'Thousand Day War' which lasted from October 1899 to June 1903.

Shortly after the 1895 revolution, elections were held and the Conservatives were successful. In the absence of the infirm and dying President, his aid, Jose Manuel Marroquin adopted a conciliatory policy towards constitutional reforms that were being demanded by the Liberals. These were refused, however, by the President, Miguel Antonio Samiemente, on his return to power. His action led to the three years' war, the longest and most disastrous of the Colombian civil wars. General Gabriel Vargas Santos was named 'the supreme commander and Provisional President' of the Liberal forces.

78, 79 When the Thousand Day War broke out in Colombia in October 1899, the government took over the issues of the private banks. They overprinted 'This note will circulate provisionally as a banknote of the National Bank in accordance with the decree of the 17th and 30th October 1899'. The Minister of the Treasury and four members of the issuing committee added their signatures

At the outset of the fighting the Liberal forces inflicted heavy losses on Government troops, known as 'the legitimates', and were winning until the Battle of Palonegro, the bloodiest and fiercest of the war. During sixteen days of non-stop fighting in March 1900, 15,000 Government troops faced 14,000 'revolutionaries'. At one stage the Government forces lost all their positions but in a last desperate attempt they charged and dispersed Santos' forces.

About this time the Liberals began to run short of funds and at the instigation of General Rafael Uribe Uribe and for the specific purpose of financing his Revolutionary Army he ordered the printing of 1, 5 and 10 peso notes. The notes, dated 15 June 1900 and depicting patriotic scenes, were printed on both sides of ordinary ruled writing paper from wooden blocks engraved by two well-known artists at the time who were on the Liberal side: Colonels Peregrino

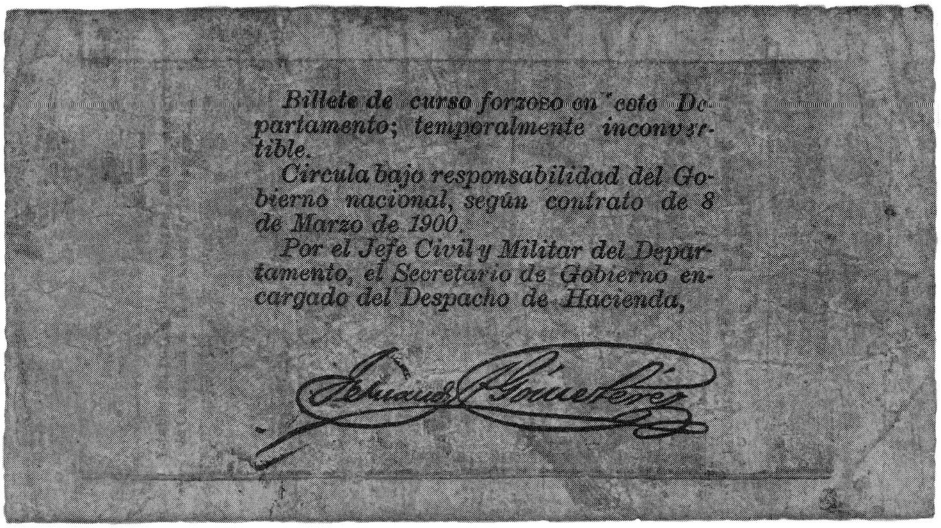

Billete de curso forzoso en este Departamento; temporalmente inconvertible.
Circula bajo responsabilidad del Gobierno nacional, según contrato de 8 de Marzo de 1900.
Por el Jefe Civil y Militar del Departamento, el Secretario de Gobierno encargado del Despacho de Hacienda,

80 Cartagena issued notes during the war under government authority overprinted on the reverse to that effect, and endorsed by the military and civil area commander

Rivera Arce and Dario Gaitan. The notes were distributed among the soldiers in the city of Ocana on the date appearing on the note. Of all the many hundreds of different emergency notes issued during the civil war these are the rarest and very few have survived.

Although some financial help came, the Liberals had to sign the 'Wisconsin' treaty in Panama on 1 June 1903. Colombia had lost over 100,000 men in this war and the economy was in chaos with a budget deficit of $800 million. There was no industry or

81 Many of the 26 provinces of Colombia issued their own notes. This note of the Banco de Santander issued at Bucaramanga in 1873 was still in use in the Thousand Day War and was overprinted in 1900

5
BANCO DE SANTANDER
Serie B
Núm.º 32534
El Banco de Santander pagará al portador, á la vista, en su oficina la suma de CINCO PESOS
BUCARAMANGA, 1º de Junio de 1873.
CINCO PESOS

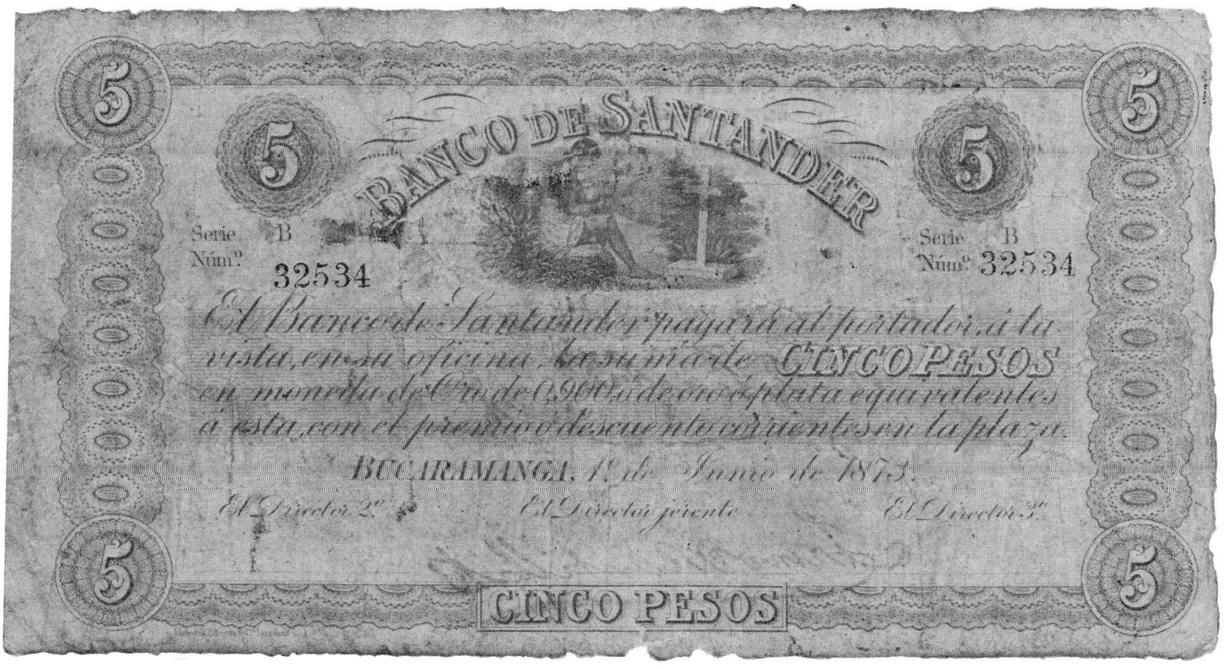

82 *The improvised notes to finance the Liberals in the Thousand Day War were issued on the initiative of Rafael Uribe Uribe, one of the generals under Santos (Lozano Collection)*

agriculture to speak of and Colombia had suffered a great loss of prestige in the eyes of the world.

One of the significant indirect consequences of this pitiful civil war was the secession of Panama from Colombia, a matter that was looked upon with anger and frustration by the Colombians. In 1906 President Theodore Roosevelt, having decided to build a canal across the isthmus of Panama, staged a further revolution in the area. The USA then intervened on the side of the revolutionaries and recognised the puppet government of Panama. Colombia, staggering in the weakness that followed this thousand-day war, had hardly the strength even to protest. It is interesting that part of the 25 million dollar indemnity paid by the USA to the Colombian Government was later used to set

up the Banco de la Republica de Colombia.

PERU

The only emergency paper money in Peru's history was issued in 1920 during the shortest revolt that the country was to experience. These were to become known among collectors as the 'Cervanteros' after the name of the leader of this revolt—Captain Guillermo Cervantes.

On 28 July 1921 Peru was about to celebrate its first centenary, and festivities were to be concentrated in the capital, Lima. At this time the Amazon city of Iquitos was in a state of depression following the collapse of the great rubber industry there. For several years it had been the boom centre of world rubber supplies but now it was being sadly neglected by the central authorities.

Money was short and amounts promised by the government to public employees and armed forces garrisoned in the town were not being paid.

The 2,000 libras which was finally received was far short of the promised amounts and insufficient to pay the wages and debts that had meanwhile accrued. It was these circumstances that led Guillermo Cervantes, head of the local battalion, to lead a rising against the government.

On 5 August 1921 Cervantes proclaimed himself the political and military head of the city and announced details of the new revolutionary structure. He accused the President, Augusto B. Leguia, of betraying the people by agreeing to cede the whole Putumayo region to the Colombians, and he accused the local authorities of holding back monies due to the soldiers. His oratory won him the support he had hoped for and he was joined by an exiled Peruvian Colonel, Teaboldo Gonzales, who made his way from Ecuador.

In order to continue his revolution, Cervantes needed money. His first action after the take-over was the confiscation of £13,000 in gold from the coffers of the local 'Bank of Peru and London'. He then issued seven denominations of notes—which he named 'Provisional Notes for Forced Circulation'—and which local inhabitants had to accept in exchange for their gold and silver possessions.

These notes were printed in a local shop, the Empresa Tipografia El Oriente, on very cheap paper. Only 4 plates were used for the 7 denominations; the lower values were all printed from the same 1 sole plate on different colour paper with the value overprinted. The highest denomination and largest note (154mm x 76mm) was the 5 libras. All the notes are

dated 1 October 1921. The signatories are Guillermo Cervantes—Captain, Military and Civil leader—and Octavio de los Heros—Administrator of Customs.

Cervantes' revolution was over within four months on 2 January 1922. The military actions against the revolutionaries were well co-ordinated. One force led by Captain G. Matos approached Iquitos from the south and the other led by Major Santibanes moved forward from the west through the Maranon river. Both these forces had several skirmishes on the way, from one of which Teobaldo Gonzales fled never to be seen again.

Cervantes, who had remained in Iquitos, was able to make good his escape by blockading the rivers with boats, thus delaying the rapidly approaching forces. He made his way to Ecuador by sailing northward on the Napo river, after which his fate is unknown.

The quantity of notes in circulation caused financial havoc but in order to normalise commerce merchants kept this currency circulating for a number of months after the revolution.

83 Cervantes' notes were printed on cheap cardboard paper, the same plate being used for the first three denominations. The value of 20 and 50 centavos was overprinted on the notes of 1 sol

ARGENTINE

Some fascinating banking history can be learned from the issues of the London

and River Plate Bank. This was the first foreign bank to open on the South American sub-continent. Under the management of J. H. Green, branches in Buenos Aires and Montevideo were opened in January 1863.

The rapid success of the bank makes an interesting story. Gold bullion for the backing of intended note issues, credit documents and other papers had been physically transported by Mr Green from London to the Argentine. A few years later the London and River Plate Bank became the first and only bank to have a gunboat come to the rescue of its managers who had been jailed by local authorities!!

The bank almost met with disaster in the first weeks of its existence when a local financial crisis led to a panic run on the bank. The enterprising Mr Green averted serious trouble by hastily arranging for the return of £40,000 in gold which had been lent to the newly formed Montevideo branch.

Real problems, however, did not begin until 1866 when the Rosario branch of the bank opened after lengthy negotiations with the Sante Fé govern-ment. The world monetary situation was adversely affecting the two rivals of the London and River Plate Bank: the Banco Nacional and the Banco de la Provincia de Santa Fé. The London bank, however, with past international experience, was successful in coping with the situation. The Banco de la Provincia was largely government-owned and the success of the English bank was an embarrassment of some concern. In addition to dis-counting bills and charging a low rate of interest on loans, the London and River Plate Bank captured the limited market with notes that were redeemable in Bolivian silver. This brought even the richest landowners to the bank for loans.

The weakening of the Provincial Bank forced the government to 'rescue' its protégé by suppressing the issue of notes redeemable in Bolivian silver. This, of course, only affected the London bank, but not to the extent hoped for by the government. The bank's business continued to improve and its services were constantly sought. During the commercial depression that settled on Rosario in the following years the banknote issues of the London and

River Plate Bank were still considered to be the most reliable.

The government, meanwhile, frustrated and still endeavouring to do something on behalf of the local banks, announced a general directive withdrawing from all banks the right to issue notes, with two exceptions: the Provincial Bank of Santa Fé and the National Bank! The same two exceptions applied to the heavy taxes which were placed on all banks. Since the London bank was the only one to suffer from these measures, the owners decided in 1875 to sue the government, simultaneously petitioning the Sante Fé President, Nicolas Avallaneda, to return to them their original rights, including the issue of banknotes.

The petition failed and the case against the government was lost. Prior to the court's decision, the London and River Plate Bank had refused even to consider proposals made by the government for amalgamation with the Provincial Bank, and this had almost led to open hostilities. The government accused the London bank of instigating a revolution, and desperately attempted to crush what it considered to be a danger to the economic stability of the province.

In May 1876, the government ordered the compulsory liquidation of the Rosario branch of the bank, but influential and important personalities in Rosario organised a petition against the decree. The government, under pressure, consented to negotiate a settlement whereby money would be lent by the London bank to its rival. While this proposal was being considered by the manager of the bank, Ludwig Behn, members of the police force broke into the bank and demanded immediate voluntary liquidation. Behn's refusal led to his imprisonment and the gold bullion in the bank was confiscated.

The next event could have led to war. The British Minister in Buenos Aires, St John, hearing of the imprisonment of Behn, ordered a British gunboat, stationed in Montevideo, to make its way towards Rosario. The threat to the Santa Fé Government was sufficient.

85 Notes of the Rosario branch of the London and River Plate Bank were issued on various dates and bear different portraits

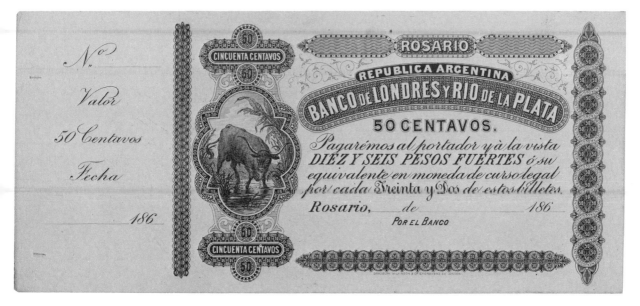

They released Ludwig Behn and undertook to make good their confiscation and safeguard the bank's interests in future. The gunboat left the Argentine coast. Unfortunately, however, the government still hoped to avoid fulfilling its undertaking. The London bank had discounted some official bills which had to be paid in gold. In order to avoid such payments, the government decreed that all bills would henceforth be payable in Provincial Bank paper currency!

At the instigation of the local managers, George Drabble, Chairman of the London and River Plate Bank, made his way to Rosario and after due consideration, and an impasse in his negotiations with Governor Bayo of Santa Fé, he decided to liquidate the bank. Business in the area had virtually stopped, income from the port and custom authorities had ceased and government revenue began to dry up.

When loans and debts were called in, public opinion once more favoured the London bank. The government was again forced to act. Finally a face-saving solution was found by Dr Hipolito Irigoyen, the Argentinian Foreign Minister, who made a loan to the Provincial Bank and the London bank accepted this currency as repayment for the debt. Within a few months, under a new manager, the London and River Plate Bank was re-established as the leading bank on the sub-continent.

In 1923, the London and River Plate Bank amalgamated with the London and Brazilian Bank to form the Bank of London and South America. Today BOLSA is still the only British bank in the Argentine.

PARAGUAY

It is tragic when a nation's economy is adversely affected by a shortage of people to spend its money! Yet this is

86 The Montevideo branch of the London and River Plate bank, faced real problems early in 1874, when the government issued its own notes and made all other currency illegal. However, the population would not accept the government paper money and the London bank, with the Banco de Commercio, survived

exactly what happened in Paraguay during the second half of the last century as a result of the disastrous War of The Triple Alliance.

Only three years after setting up its own government Paraguay found itself under the severe dictatorship of Dr J. G. R. Francia in 1814. During the 26 years of his leadership he built and consolidated Paraguay's independence and with the help of Carlos Antonio Lopez, who was to succeed him in 1840, he developed a strong and powerful army. When Lopez became president, boundary disputes with neighbouring Brazil and Argentina began and continued until Carlos Lopez was succeeded by his son, Francisco Solano Lopez, in 1862.

The young Lopez adopted a stringent foreign policy and, with the still powerful Paraguayan Army, did not hesitate in 1864 to declare war on Brazil, siding with the Uruguayan Nationalist where Brazil was already involved in the civil war. His action brought about the unification of Brazilian, Uruguayan and Argentinian forces who invaded Paraguay early in 1865 to overthrow Lopez and settle the longstanding border disputes on their own terms.

The five years of war that followed saw the absolute defeat of the Paraguayans and the death of Lopez on 1 March 1870. Paraguay had recruited every able-bodied person into active service. Battalions of women and twelve-year-old boys had been formed and these were annihilated. Over one million men, women and children had been killed and of the remaining population only some 30,000 were men!

Paraguay issued its first paper money at the beginning of the war in 1865. It is for sad reasons that these early notes can still be easily obtained by collectors.

87 The earliest notes issued by Paraguay were undated but are reported to have entered circulation only a short time before the tragic 1865 War. These notes are now probably the easiest of the early South American notes to be obtained

7: Inflation

CHINA

China experienced paper inflation before most countries of the world had even heard about paper money, let alone used it! The Mongols, needing more and more money to bolster their extended empire, resorted to the printing press. The results of unbacked money have become familiar throughout history.

During the early part of the twentieth century China experienced a form of inflation once again. It must be remembered that during the Ming Dynasty paper money was abolished. It did not appear again until the Tai-Ping rebellion, when emergency notes were printed. But now the war lords issued paper money on a different principle.

It was simply made known that anyone not using it would be considered unpatriotic, a traitor and liable to a severe penalty. (A severe penalty in China in the 1920s was a prompt be-heading.) So paper money circulated widely in China at a time when in the West paper was solidly backed by gold and silver. The Chinese warlords had a substitute for gold and silver which was just as effective—the cold steel of their soldiers' swords!

War with Japan and finally involvement in World War II saw inflation sweep through China on a scale that dwarfed the Mongol inflation of centuries before. Different types of paper money were issued and their inflationary history can be traced by the steady rise in denominations. A good example is the Customs Gold Unit. These notes were originally introduced to pay customs import duties. When first brought in they were backed by 60 per cent gold reserves—which is much better backing than the paper currency of any nation in the world has today! First issued in 1931 they lasted until 1937 with reasonable efficiency—the total issued rising from 250,000 CGU to 409,630 CGU. However, the Chinese Nationalists, then forced into Chungking, suddenly ceased to issue annual accounts for these units and equally suddenly very large denominations began to appear. Although many of these were printed as late as 1946, they all carry the original date of 1930—the Chinese authorities taking the view that this tended to show that the notes were not inflationary and had always existed for high amounts!

By 1948 the fractional notes of CGU were a standing joke and the higher denominations included notes for 25,000, 50,000 and 250,000. The currency reform of 1948 swept them away and achieved a record by nearly doubling the existing currency within two months, from 70,000,000 million to 135,000,000 million Chinese National Currency dollars.

A new currency, the gold yuan was introduced in 1948, though some were dated 1945. Here again the issues provide a fine example of galloping inflation. Starting at a mere 10 cents, they rose to a million gold yuan by 1949 with no less than 34 different designs of notes. China for all its size could not produce the amount needed, and gold yuan notes were printed, often within the same year, by Thomas De La Rue, London; Central Trust Press, Shanghai; American Banknote Co, New York; Chungwha Book Co, Shanghai; Ta Tung Book Co, Shanghai; and the Central Printing Co, Shanghai.

Initially the government had promised that gold yuan would be 100 per cent backed by gold and that no notes above 100 gold yuan would be issued. Within a year of issue notes for a million were circulating and were soon to become worthless.

88 *The reverse of the customs gold unit note of the Central Bank of China. These were dated 1930 although some were issued as late as 1946*

The government switched from gold to silver and introduced the Central Bank's Silver Certificate. It was decreed that silver yuan certificates would be freely redeemed in silver coin on demand. Where silver coins were inadequate to meet demand they could be redeemed in gold. Mao Tse Tung, however, had a disastrous effect on their value and eventually the notes were not even worth the paper they were printed on.

RUSSIA
Russia suffered serious inflation in the

aftermath of World War I and today much of its colourful paper money is still available to collectors at very low prices.

Wars cost money and when Russia became involved in hostilities in 1914 the printing press was resorted to. In the early part of 1914 something like 1,633 million roubles were in circulation. By August this figure had reached 2,431 million and by September, 2,642 million.

Gold and silver had disappeared completely and the situation worsened to such an extent that a Bank Moratorium was introduced, freezing all accounts in Russia of over 100 roubles. An individual was allowed to draw only five per cent of his balance per month and in no event was he allowed to draw more than 500 roubles a month.

In an attempt at stabilisation the authorities issued banknotes with dates as early as 1898—the idea was that people should think the currency sound and long-lasting. In fact the notes can only be accurately dated by the name of the state bank director who signed them. More notes dated 1910 were in fact issued during the revolution than were actually issued in 1910!

This was the situation inherited by the Provisional Government which came into existence on 2 March 1917. Its attempts to resolve the desperate position were abortive. The giant working class of Russia, represented through the Soviet of Workers and Soldiers Deputies, staged strikes and demonstrations, and eventually, on 5 May 1917, forced a coalition government.

Lenin demanded that the Provisional Government should be transferred to the Soviets. General Kornilov was instructed to march with his army to destroy Lenin's forces, but the attack was cancelled when it was found that more than 40,000 workers had joined Lenin at Petrograd.

At the head of the Provisional Government Kerensky was doomed. Not only was his position hopeless because of the social reforms demanded by Lenin and his followers, but his financial system was collapsing. The war debt alone was a staggering 30,000 million roubles and by the beginning of March 1917 the paper rouble was worth in fact only 27 kopecks.

Even so, more and more paper money was needed. Russian printing presses were not capable of meeting the demand and British and American printing firms were contracted to do the work.

Beautifully produced notes were introduced as well as roughly printed ones, and the Russians, used to the magnificently engraved notes of the Czars, often would refuse to accept the badly printed notes. But nothing could assuage the appetite of the Russian population for paper money. Towards the end the Provisional Government was reduced to circulating notes without serial numbers or signatures—and finally in complete uncut sheets! The uncut

89 The Provisional Government had already collapsed when a shipload of these notes arrived in Russia. Printed by the American Banknote Co, they were eventually put into circulation without signatures or serial numbers

sheets were quickly nicknamed 'beer stamps' and the Minister of Finance made a public statement that they were only temporary and would soon be replaced with good-quality notes. Before this, however, the Provisional Government fell.

The notes printed in America consisted of 50 kopecks, 25, 50, 100, 250, 500 and 1,000 roubles and bonds. The bonds were for 200 roubles each and many were subsequently overprinted for use as currency notes—others circulated as currency even without the overprint.

90 A Russian bond printed for the Provisional Government but used by its successors as actual currency notes

The Provisional Government was overthrown before the printing consignment arrived at Vladivostock. Probably much to the annoyance of the American Banknote Co, the notes were subsequently used by the new authorities, the White Guard Government of Admiral Kolchak, which used the 50 kopecks without signature. The government of the maritime region used the same notes but overprinted 'Ivanov'. The bonds fell into the hands of, among others, the Russian Socialist Federal Soviet Republic, and the Siberian Revolutionary Committee made them legal tender.

At this time there were many foreign troops engaged in the struggle for power in Russia—British, American, French, Czechoslovakian, Rumanian, Greek, Japanese and many more. Enormous quantities of paper money were needed to finance these armies and the generals and admirals often issued notes themselves. Among the more common issues are those of General Wrangel, General Deikan and Admiral Kolchak.

Admiral Kolchak was appointed Supreme Commander of the All Russian Government and into his care was placed the national gold reserve of Russia. This travelled with him by railway. But his harsh treatment of his soldiers — mainly Czech — led to his downfall. As the Red Army moved from victory to victory Kolchak's own soldiers arrested him and imprisoned him to await trial. On 7 February 1920 he was given a 'drumhead' trial and shot dead.

To add to the financial confusion there were territories which did not ally themselves to either the Red Army or the White Army, and these issued their own notes. More than 400 cities issued their own paper money to make up for the total lack of coins. Restaurants, parent teachers associations, Society of Consumers and so on all issued notes for small change.

Finally notes were appearing in some sectors for millions of roubles and had no greater value than the original 50 kopecks! The giant-sized 100 and 500 rouble notes which depict Catherine and Peter the Great became worthless. Many of the nobility had brought them out of Russia by the suitcase full and now found themselves penniless. Only now are these beautiful notes finding some value—among collectors of old bank-notes.

GERMANY

Possibly the only benefit derived from inflation is the maze of colourful paper money issues which have become available to collectors! During the inflationary period in Germany after World War I emergency notes were being issued by towns and cities throughout the country.

Inflation had been soaring since 1919 and by mid-1922 it had reached such proportions that certain employees were being paid wages twice a day in order to keep up with the increasing cost of daily necessities. It was, however, the serious shortage of small change that led towns and cities to issue their own notes. These were known as *notgeld*, and they were issued in such huge quantities at a face value so low that a large number of people began to collect them. As soon as this was realised by the municipalities involved, special issues began to appear depicting local scenes, with patriotic slogans, portraits and often poems and propaganda texts directed at tourists.

The total number of *notgeld* issues is quite fantastic. It has been recorded that some 3,500 cities issued a total of almost 50,000 different notes between 1914 and 1922. On 17 September 1922 a general prohibition was placed on the issue of private notes—although some were still printed in order to satisfy the 10,000 or more collectors of these issues.

In spite of this there was no improvement in the economic situation and the Reichsbank had to permit additional issues of *notgeld* by towns and cities.

92 Czarist notes were used by the Revolutionaries who freely printed from the original plates. They can only be dated correctly by the signatures found on them. This note shows Peter the Great on the reverse. It was to become worthless

These new emergency issues became known as cheque notes since they were backed by the bank and this fact was stated on the text of the note. The value of the mark continued to drop and eventually 30,000 people and over 80 private printing houses were employed in keeping up with the increased demand

93, 94, 95 Germany suffered one of the worst inflations of the twentieth century. All coin disappeared and almost every town and city in Germany issued its own notes. First they produced notgeld emergency notes for small change and finally notes for multi-millions of marks

for paper money. At this time many of the earlier German issues were also overprinted, some of them twice on the same note! The highest denomination was the 100 billion mark, which at the time was equivalent to £7 sterling.

The *rentenmark* was Germany's saviour. The idea of Karl Helffich, this new unit was introduced in 1924 and was based on the monetary reforms which had solved Danish problems during the Napoleonic inflation.

HUNGARY

The inflation which raged through Germany in 1922/23 was serious enough in itself, but even greater was the Hungarian 'hyper-inflation' which followed immediately after World War II.

Hungary suffered severe economic problems during the war and the trend of inflation persisted throughout. In 1944 two billion pengos were circulating within the country; this was a four-fold increase on the currency in circulation two years earlier.

It was a classic economic situation: a continually decreasing availability of consumer goods; government attempts to cover its deficits by increasing its paper money issues; and the resulting lack of public confidence in the pengo.

The shortage of equipment and skilled labour prevented the Hungarian Finance Ministry from reissuing banknotes immediately after the end of the war. This was only done after the ministry had obtained, in July 1944, loans from the Russians which allowed for the issue of postwar notes.

Soon after the first issue, additional notes were issued in ever increasing quantities. And in December 1945 a levy worth 75 per cent of the face value of the banknote was placed on some issues in the form of a stamp. This

96 The German inflation brought about high denomination notes during 1922 and 1923. This note is for 20 million marks

lasted for two weeks.

The pengo denomination had, by the beginning of 1946, undergone such inflation that it had to be replaced by the milpengo, which equalled 1,000 old pengos. These were issued from March until June 1946 when this unit too had to be replaced by the bil-pengo, equivalent to 1,000,000,000,000 of the old pengo! On 9 July 1946 a new monetary unit had once more to be introduced. This was the adopengo which in English may be translated as 'tax pengo'. Although this was originally issued in order to facilitate the collection of government taxes, it only slightly affected the continuing inflation and was soon a popular form of exchange instead of the

97 Turned on its side, this note of the inflation period has a hidden drawing — a vampire at the throat of the young German. It was a reference to the harshness of the Versailles Treaty which many Germans contended was 'bleeding the country dry'

98, 99 *Postwar inflation in Hungary rose so high that instead of adding 'o', the issuers changed the names of the type of pengo*

previous bil-pengo. Here too, within two weeks the ratio of the increase of the adopengo was 4,400 to one and four weeks later 108,000 to one.

The inflation reached its climax between 25 May 1946 and 31 July of that year, after additional measures such as auxiliary legal tender stamps and treasury notes of the Hungarian postal savings bank circulated in all sorts of denominations. The new monetary unit was to be the forint (last used in the 1850s) which on 1 August 1946 was equivalent to 200 million adopengo. Some of these 1945/46 notes make a most beautiful selection of artistic engraving, and are quite easy for collectors to obtain.

GREECE

Modern Greek currency dates back only to 1828, the year of Greece's independence from Turkish Rule. From this date Greece, probably more than most ancient nations, has preserved its old tradition and endeavoured to incorporate it into the modern state. This has been particularly evident on the paper money issues of Greece from 1831, when the first banknotes appeared. These notes have reflected Greece's great past with pictures from history and mythology, personalities, gods, architecture, and ancient Greek coins.

The economic humiliation suffered by Greece in World War II at the hands of the Italians and Germans was twofold. The intention of the occupation forces was to circulate currency in such quantities as to assure the nation's financial ruin. The Italian forces occupying Greece in 1940 were the first to issue bilingual notes in the territories. Aware of the importance of the past to the Greeks they decided to portray legendary figures. But they erred and produced notes on which Jupiter (the Roman counterpart of the great Greek god) instead of Zeus appeared!

The Italian offensive against Greece began on 27 October 1940 and by 6 April 1941, when the Germans attacked in order to aid their defeated allies, the paper money issues in the country had

100 A 'B' pengo with denomination 100,000 in fact meant 100,000,000,000,000,000!

101, 102, 103 The wartime inflation in Greece was intentionally brought about by the Germans and the Italians. The bottom note is the highest denomination of this series and is equivalent to 10 billion drachmas

ΤΡΑΠΕΖΑ ΤΗΣ ΕΛΛΑΔΟΣ

100.000   100.000

ΕΚΔΟΣΙΣ ΠΡΩΤΗ

104 All the Greek inflation notes had beautiful designs and depictions. This note shows the reverse of the 100,000 drachmas 1944 issue

already increased by 50 per cent. From that date onward a chronic state of inflation developed which is witnessed by the rate of exchange established on 11 November 1944, the date of Greece's liberation by the British.

The economic ruin of Greece which the Axis forces deliberately contrived was not limited to the monetary system of the country. The Germans were determined to drain Greece of all its wealth. Roads, railway lines, ports and fields were systematically destroyed; disease and devastation settled on the country and jewels, coins and national treasures were transported in train loads out of the country.

The official Greek reports on the tremendous loss to the country quote crippling figures. The total damage to the national economy was in excess of 320 million English gold sovereigns. The country's income during and after the war was nil and over 300 million dollars worth of war material had been lost. The country had lost its wealth of metals and minerals on which the economy had relied in the past and was now in financial ruin. With the help of the allied forces and a strong determination Greece recovered and the first notes issued by the liberation government depicted the Phoenix. It was a symbol of the return to independence.

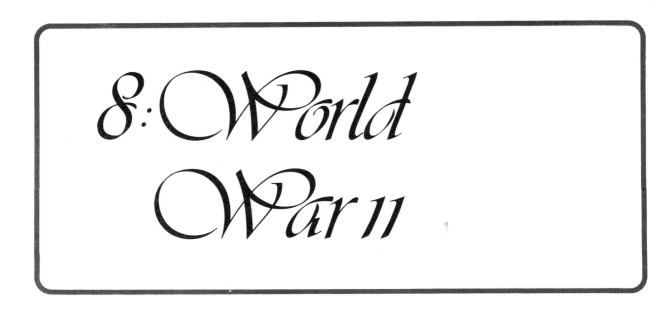

8: World War II

Paper money owes its existence to emergency situations. Gold and silver had an intrinsic value which the receiver understood, but a note was 'not worth the paper it was written on', unless the writing could be trusted. So there had to be a real emergency before a man would take paper instead of gold and he had to be persuaded of its validity.

Fortunately for the issuers of paper money, people generally tend not to study history too closely, for vast amounts of paper money throughout history have become worthless, the issuers failing to honour them and the holder finding that paper had no intrinsic value like precious metals.

World War II provided the greatest emergency situation and need for paper money, and vast quantities were issued between 1939 and 1945. New types of paper money were introduced and the history of the war can be traced through banknote issues.

AXIS POWERS

Germany, the mainstay of Axis power, paid the same thorough attention to its wartime paper money as it did to all military problems. If the whirlwind advance of German troops through Europe confused everyone else it did not confuse the banknote printers who were ready and soon efficiently supplying the paper needs of its conquering forces. Several types of paper money came into use.

There were the *Reichskreditkassen* notes for circulation in occupied countries. By order of the Supreme Army Commander dated 23 September 1939 they were authorised as currency and on 2 October 1939, while bitter fighting still raged in Poland, they were put into circulation in that territory. The *Reichskreditkassen*, which ranged from

50 pfennig to 50 marks, were subsequently to see service in Belgium, Denmark, Greece, France, Luxembourg, Norway, Russia and Yugoslavia, as well as the British islands of Jersey and Guernsey.

The German soldiers had their own special paper money. The Auxiliary Payment Certificate (*Behelfszahlungsmittel*) more than paid for the cost of their issue. They were for the use of German soldiers in canteens and barracks all over Axis-controlled territory. The only difference between these notes and normal banknotes was that they were valued at ten times the face value. So a civilian receiving a 10 Reichmark had to give the soldier ten times its value in goods or services. When, however, he subsequently presented the note for redemption the German authorities paid him the face value!

The British were not slow to make capital of this. They forged the notes, which have blank reverses, and printed

'poems' on the backs—some extremely rude—generally pointing out that the whole thing was a swindle. The RAF dropped them over Germany's allies.

Encouraged by the success of the issue the Germans soon thought up another idea. These were the *Verrechnungsscheine* (reckoning notes) and the idea was that German soldiers leaving for duty in occupied territories would be given these to cash in the occupied territory for the notes in use in that place.

105 20 mark Reichskreditkassen (*Reich credit note*)

106 Behelfszahlungsmittel notes which were forged by the British with messages on the reverse

107 *A 6d note issued in Jersey during the German occupation*

Because of the difficulties and costs of transport some areas were allowed to print their own emergency notes. These included Guernsey and Jersey who in 1941 began producing small denomination notes. Guernsey issued 6d notes in 1941 and other notes in shilling denominations. Taking advantage of the printing facilities, the Channel Islanders, under the noses of German sentries, printed notes dated 1945 for £1 which, within hours of the German surrender, were in circulation as Channel Island notes. They earned the islanders a commendation from the Bank of England for being the first occupied territory to resume normal banking issues.

As the war progressed and prisoners of war were captured in large numbers it became necessary to provide special paper money for them. A general issue was soon printed for use by the Wehrmacht in all military prison camps. Although a large number were issued at the time these notes, which carry a coloured triangle in the centre, are now very scarce indeed. Sometimes these notes are found with rubber stamps on

the backs showing the camp in which they were used. Over 60 such camps have been identified.

The Italians also issued special war notes. But unlike the Germans they found very little use for them. Indeed, two out of the three main 'occupation' issues printed, never saw the light of day because the soldiers were not in a position to ensure their circulation. These were the occupation notes for Egypt, 'Cassa Mediterranea di Credito Per L'Egitto' showing a handsome vignette of Julius Caesar, and the 'Cassa Mediterranea di Credito Per il Sudan'. Mussolini had intended to split Egypt into two, Egypt to have Cairo as its capital and the Sudan to have Khartoum. In both cases the notes had to be destroyed when the military failed to implement the plans. But Italian occupation notes did circulate in Greece, 'Cassa Mediterranea di credito Per La Grecia,' and also in the Ionian islands.

From time to time the Axis powers were obliged to make use of existing banknotes, as in Poland which continued fighting for some time. Notes were overprinted in red 'Generalgouvernement für die besetzten polnischen Gebiete' (Occupied Polish Territories).

The war also saw new states created and a flood of new paper money for them. Such a state was Croatia, whose notes can be identified by the word 'Hrvatska'. These notes were printed by the German firm, Giesecke and Devrient, and issued from May 1941 to January 1944.

YUGOSLAVIA

Yugoslavia was occupied, but never truly suppressed, by German forces in World War II. Evidence of the Yugoslavs' remaining control over their affairs is clearly demonstrated in the

paper money of the time. Indeed, as far as South Slovenia was concerned, the partisan issues were the only legal tender notes and the people avoided using other notes whenever possible.

At the end of the war the Yugoslav Ministry of Information released details of notes presented in 1945 for exchange into the new dinar currency. They included a total of 260 million partisan notes!

The Wehrmacht invaded Yugoslavia on 6 April 1941, and within a fortnight the Yugoslav army was obliged to surrender. General Milan Nedic established a puppet regime and Germany and Italy divided the territory between them.

But almost immediately two separate partisan forces were set up, neither of which were successfully quelled by the Germans. On occasion the two powerful 'armies' fought each other as well as the Germans. They were the Cetnik forces led by Draja Mihailovic, who were conservative in politics, and the communist forces led by Josip Broz (Marshal Tito), who were regularly supplied by Russia. The Western Allies supported both partisan armies until 1944 when, as Tito had gained such an ascendency, they swallowed their pride and threw their full weight behind Tito—with the result that to this day the communist regime of Yugoslavia enjoys cordial relations with the West.

There were many small issues of notes made by the partisans under difficult circumstances but their organisation was so good that in June 1944 they made substantial issues for the liberated areas. The Economic Finance Committee of the Liberation Front for the Slovenian People also issued 'Liberty Loan' notes which, although bonds rather than banknotes, were soon freely used as legal tender. The Denarni Zavod Slovenije issues carried the message: 'Death to Fascism'.

MONTENEGRO

During the war Yugoslavian notes circulated in Montenegro and, after the German forces had subdued military resistance there, they handed the territory over to Italy.

The Montenegrins caused the Italians more trouble with existing note issues than they did with partisan issues. The Italian forces were astonished to see how rich all the peasants were until it was discovered how they obtained the money. Government officials had fled at the approach of the German Army, taking with them truckloads of banknotes from the national bank safes. As they reached the mountains it was found that the trucks could no longer negotiate the rough terrain, so the truckloads of notes were hidden in mountain caves before the government continued its escape on foot.

But all this had not gone unnoticed by the wily peasants who distributed all the notes before the Axis forces came on the scene.

To overcome the situation the Italians required all notes to be handed in and, having obtained from the main bank the serial numbers of notes officially put into circulation, checked the notes off individually. Those that had been in normal circulation were overstamped 'Verificato' (verified) and returned; the rest were destroyed. Many Montenegrins merely overstamped their own notes—and took the opportunity to overstamp earlier issues that had been out of circulation for some time and were not redeemable any more. These they passed on to the occupation troops.

The Montenegro partisans also issued their own notes, dominated by the red star of Russia. The notes were 'diminishing in value', meaning that each month they were worth less—a method of ensuring circulation. Three denominations are known—10 dinar, 100 dinar and 1,000 dinar—all showing partisans.

GREECE

The Civil Committee for National

109 A Yugoslavian note circulated in Montenegro and 'verified' by the Italian occupation authorities

Liberation, controlled by partisans in Northern Greece, made one large issue of notes on 5 June 1944 which were used to buy provisions for the partisan army. Four denominations were issued and the notes depict a partisan soldier with rifle. Immediately after the war the Greeks published a booklet collection of Greek war notes together with quotations from the Allies about their defiant opposition to the Germans: 'Formerly we used to say: The Greeks are battling like heroes; now we may say: The Heroes are battling like Greeks'—BBC London 28 October 1942; 'On the 28 of October, an ultimatum expiring in three hours, not in three days or weeks, was given to Greece. But had it been three years the answer would have still been the same'—Franklin D. Roosevelt 10 June 1945.

JAPAN

The Japanese were also very active during the war in the issue of paper money.

The Japanese Army notes are probably the most attractive of all war issues. Known to collectors as 'Bird and Dragon' notes they are excellent examples of Japanese art. But ordinary Japanese paper money was also overprinted for military use—extremely rare are those Japanese notes with small violet overprinted circles containing characters. They were used in emergency circumstances in Hongkong and sometimes the overprints can be very difficult to see.

Apart from the Army notes, the Japanese issued occupation notes in such profusion that towards the end of the war Japanese pay officers used measuring sticks to pay their troops, as to count the notes was impractical. Inflation had made a mockery of Japanese dollars. The occupation notes can easily be identified by the English wording—'The Japanese Government'. The country for which the note was intended can be identified by the first serial letter. A note with

110 The dragon design, which is one of the most attractive of the wartime Japanese banknotes

111 *A Japanese army note for 10 yen*

112 *The only notes issued by the Japanese in sterling were those for 'Oceania'*

serial 'MA 646211' would be Malaya—similarly, B=Burma, O=Oceania, and P=Philippines. The Oceania notes were the only Japanese notes ever to be issued in sterling denominations and generally they are scarcer than the dollar issues. They were used in New Guinea, Gilbert Islands and Solomon Islands and were issued in denominations of ½ shilling, 1 shilling, 10 shillings and 1 pound.

Most famous and also most common of the Japanese occupation notes is the Malaya 10 dollar note showing banana trees. This was very quickly nicknamed 'banana money' and 'Mickey Mouse money' by British prisoners of war.

THE JAPANESE GOVERNMENT
PROMISES TO PAY THE BEARER
ON DEMAND
ONE HUNDRED
DOLLARS
MT MT
100 100
100 100

113 100 dollar note issued by the Japanese for the occupation of Malaya

Collectors owe the existence of a great many of these notes to a daring robbery. American combat troops fought their way into Manila, the capital of the Philippines and set up an emergency battle headquarters in a large mainstreet building. As a matter of routine troops were sent to explore neighbouring buildings. They found that the building opposite was the depository for Japanese occupation notes and was stuffed full of them, ready for issue to any of the occupied territories. A guard was hastily put round the building. Nevertheless, a group of American jungle troops put their training to good use by breaking into the building and helping themselves to enormous quantities.

As the whole area was still under battle conditions the authorities had more important matters to attend to and the robbery was a success. This explains why collectors can still buy 100 dollar occupation bills for about 25 pence.

The American government itself was not particularly interested in the cache because they had forged the occupation notes in vast quantities anyway, and General Douglas MacArthur wrote in his memoirs that his ability to have unrestricted access to 'occupation reproductions' was a considerable advantage.

The Japanese operated their own bank in occupied China by setting up a puppet state under a pro-Japanese government in Shanghai. The Central Reserve Bank of China was established in December 1940 and issued a long and colourful set of notes. The Chinese engravers, however, were often very anti-Japanese and one inserted 'hidden' English letters in the scroll work of the 200 yuan note of 1944. The letters, 'U.S.A.C.' were to represent 'United States Army Coming'. This note naturally offended the Japanese and was hurriedly withdrawn, the engraver being executed.

The Japanese also set up the Federal Reserve Bank of China and their wartime occupation notes include some of great beauty. The 'sky dragon' notes

行銀備儲央中

M391033AE   M391033AE

貳百圓   貳百圓

中華民國國幣貳百圓
中華民國三十三年印

114 200 yuan of the Federal Reserve Bank of China containing the secret letters 'U.S.A.C.' (United States Army Coming)

were given much earlier Chinese bank-note designs which had not been used.

The Japanese, like the Germans, had their problems with partisans and were faced with guerilla currencies. For the inhabitants to be caught in possession of such money meant instant decapitation. The Philippines produced more guerilla notes than any other occupied territory, and there are something like a hundred different Philippine guerilla notes which have so far come into the hands of collectors. It will be remembered that the Philippines maintained a continual struggle against the Japanese even after the occupation of their land. In the maze of small islands guerillas would make their own notes which the local inhabitants accepted out of patriotism—even though possession of such notes meant immediate execution if the Japanese caught them.

Notes are known which were printed with wood-blocks, typewriters and even engraved on the casings of old rubber

tyres. The paper varies from wrapping paper to the backs of printed documents.

Most of these notes were redeemed at face value by the Philippine Government at the end of the war. Those that turn up now come from hoards that were hidden away from the Japanese and never recovered.

There were two major note issues in the Philippines. The 'Guingona' issue was printed before the Japanese invaded Mindanao, and a navy lieutenant, Sam Wilson, who had been an engraver in Manila when war broke out, was responsible. Before the fall of Bataan he was sent to Visayas and then to Mindanao to carry out the engraving and printing. Guingona was the Commissioner of Mindanao.

At this time there was a large sum of regular Philippine notes in the hands of the government. They were in four giant wooden cases and Guingona and Wilson took half each into their custody. Guingona buried his, but a Moro chieftain found out about it, had them dug up and they appeared with embarrassing frequency. Lieutenant Wilson held on to his half for as long as he dared, but finally, in the presence of naval witnesses, burned the lot.

The Saguin Mindanao emergency issue of notes came between 1943 and 1945 from the Currency Board under the chairmanship of Judge Florentino Saguin. On more than one occasion the 'mint' had to be moved to avoid capture and certain execution at the hands of the Japanese.

115 A guerilla currency note of the Philippines, issued by the Mindanao Emergency Currency Board

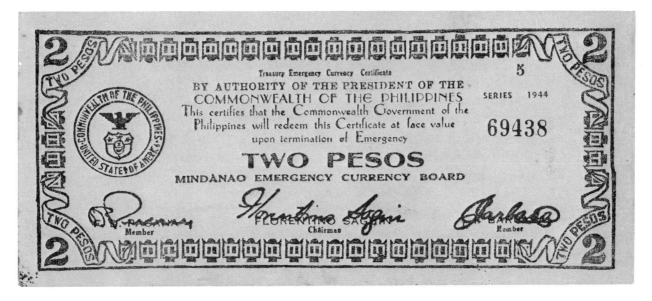

ALLIED POWERS

The Allies were almost as prolific as the Axis powers in their use of special war notes. A general issue of prisoner of war notes was made headed 'Prisoners of War Camps' and 'available in camp of issue only'. The reverse contained circles for official stamps and date marks. The Free French issued their own notes in French Equatorial Africa and French territories not under Axis administration, or Vichy France.

Several issues of paper money were made by the British government for invasion and occupation purposes. Notes issued by the British Military Authority for Tripolitania were used in the North African invasion and were in lire denominations. British Army notes for North Africa and Greece were in use between 1943 and 1945, and these were in sterling denominations from 3d to £1. Both these issues have as their centre vignette the lion passant on crown.

At the close of the war the British had currency problems in Burma and to offset this many notes bearing the head of George VI were overprinted 'Military Administration of Burma—legal tender in Burma only'. Other notes titled 'Military Administration of Burma' are known to exist.

Like the Germans the British had special money for use in canteens and NAAFI centres—but unlike the Germans there was no differential in the face value and the actual value a civilian had to give for it. These notes are simply

headed 'British Armed Forces' and range from 3d to £5.

But perhaps the most interesting of all wartime notes are the invasion issues of the Allies. The invasion of France on 'D' Day, 6 June 1944, saw the most massive military and naval operation ever mounted. Every contingency was planned for, including the issue of paper money. The notes printed ready for the occasion were inscribed 'Emis en France' (issued in France), and this caused a rumpus. General de Gaulle took exception to the fact that a tricolour appeared on the reverse—contending that only

France could authorise the use of the tricolour—and also to the 'Issued in France', which was not true.

The issue continued in use despite the French objection but when the time came for new printings the issue was changed and the offending words and flag omitted.

Similar notes were issued for Germany when the time came to enter German territory. By now there were millions of Allied troops on the continent and Britain, Russia and the United States all printed these notes using identical plates. Recent information shows that all American notes bear a mint mark 'f' on the lower right corner of small denominations and on the upper right corner of the higher denominations, standing for Forbes printing company.

A similar series was issued for Italy as early as 1943 and some forgeries very quickly appeared. Forgers were altering 50 and 100 lire notes to read 500 and 1000 respectively, with considerable success. Incidentally, allied military currency for Japan and Okinawa continued in use until 1958.

117 One of the small denomination invasion notes which annoyed General De Gaulle

Among the scarcer Allied currency are the Netherlands Liberation notes. These were extremely well printed by the American Bank Note Co, and put into circulation on 4 February 1943. They showed a portrait of Queen Wilhemenia. But the Dutch, like De Gaulle preferred to issue their own paper money and by order of the Dutch government the notes were withdrawn after only ninety days of circulation.

Russia issued its own notes for China and some European countries independently of the other Allies. These were Red Army notes and appeared in China, Korea, Czechoslovakia, Hungary, Poland, Rumania, and Manchuria.

Currency for Hong Kong was printed under emergency conditions in September 1945 and the electric power from a submarine was used for one printing. Captured banknotes from the Central Reserve Bank of China dated 1944 and 1945 were overprinted 'Hong Kong Government' and the denomination of $5 or $10. These overprints were made in Kowloon but it is doubtful if the notes ever circulated as Hong Kong notes showing George VI's portrait were flown out from England before the emergency notes were ready for circulation.

There were, of course, many other types of Allied paper money. In Belgium notes were issued headed 'Armee Belge'; Danish notes were overprinted for the Faroe Islands. One interesting issue was the printing of 1d notes in the Fiji islands. This came about because servicemen took all the coins out of circulation as keepsakes and the government of Fiji was faced with a severe shortage of small change. They issued 1d, 1s and 2s notes.

CONCENTRATION CAMPS
Litzmannstadt

The Polish city of Lodz, which was called 'Litzmannstadt' by the Germans had, like other European cities, its Jewish ghetto. This ghetto, however, was to be used by the Germans for the

118 Well-printed notes were put into circulation immediately American troops occupied the Netherlands. But after only 90 days they were withdrawn and replaced by Dutch issues

119 While Russia went along with the other Allies with some currency occupation issues, special Red Army notes were circulated in parts of China, Hungary and Czechoslovakia. This is a 20 korun note of 1944

120 The rarest of the Litzmannstadt concentration camp notes is the 50 mark denomination

internment of all the Jewish population of Poland as well as the Jewish intelligentsia of other European countries occupied by the Germans. The Lodz area was closed off in May 1940 and 300,000 Jews were held in the camp by the autumn of 1941. At the end of the war only 887 Jews had survived the extermination.

The Jews were given limited autonomy by the Germans. The ghetto had its own currency and its own post office which issued stamps. Due to a shortage of small currency a Jewish mint was set up on the initiative of the ghetto Chief Elder M. Rumkowski, and local coins were made. The notes, of different colours and in 7 denominations, all have the Star of David and a Menorah on them. The Nazis prohibited the use of German currency, thus all the notes were headed 'Quittung' meaning 'receipt' for the money that had been taken away from them.

Buchenwald

The Nazi obsession with Aryan blood and its conception of the purity of race had its most telling effects on the masses of 'non-Aryan' Slavs and Jews whose systematic extermination in concentration camps in Germany, Austria and Poland formed the basis of the 'Final Solution' advocated by Hitler from the days before the war.

In Buchenwald as in other camps the Nazi SS was as meticulous with the comfort of its officers as with the maltreatment of the inmates of the camps. Garrison canteens were set up, and officers of the SS were issued with 'vouchers' of different values. These could only be used in the canteen and one presumes that they were not convertible into ordinary currency. The denominations issued in Buchenwald were for 0.50RM, 1RM and 2RM, all printed on different coloured paper of the same size. It is claimed that the burnt edges of the notes witness the attempts of the Nazis to obliterate the evidence of such camps. The notes were found by the Allied forces with a large quantity of other semi-burnt documents.

Theresienstadt

To the south of Lodz, the Germans were planning a similar camp at Theresien-

stadt, in what was then Bohemia (now Czechoslovakia).

While Litzmanstadt had a mint of its own, Theresienstadt established its own 'Jewish Self-Government Bank'. This camp was set up to show the world how fairly the Jews were being treated by the Nazis! The majority of some 100,000 inhabitants of the ghetto were Jewish personalities, whose disappearance could have posed embarrassing questions; consequently the camp was set up as a model settlement showing humane treatment of the inhabitants who were supposedly self governed.

The first Chief Elder, Jakob Edelstein, was charged with the preparation of a set of notes which were 'receipts', and which were meant for circulation in the camp. It is interesting to note that the original designs submitted to the Nazi's were not approved. These showed Moses holding the Ten Commandments and they were not approved because Moses looked 'too Aryan'! As a result the portrait was altered by a German

designer in Berlin. He added curls to Moses hair and altered the nose into a 'more typically Jewish feature'.

The notes have different colours and bear the Star of David on the obverse. The Nazis had more difficulties in Theresienstadt in introducing the notes than they had in Litzmanstadt. When the Jewish community failed to use the notes for everyday business, the Germans at first imposed an unprecedented 'free time tax' on the inhabitants. Later, confiscated property was placed on sale at inflated prices. Members of the community saw items which originally belonged to them placed on sale for prices which they could not possibly afford to pay! All the Germans' efforts were to no avail. The system was a failure and the currency never saw proper circulation. The only practical purpose for which it was used was card games.

Of the many concentration camps established by the Nazis during the war, Litzmannstadt and Theresienstadt were

123, 124 *Theresienstadt notes. The original vignette of Moses and the Tablet of the Law was 'doctored' by a Berlin engraver to make him look less Aryan*

exceptional in that they were the only ones where the Jews had some autonomy and a supposedly normal way of life. The sets of notes issued in these two ghettoes are evidence of that.

Sachsenhausen

One concentration camp stands out for its historic attempt to forge British bank-notes: Sachsenhausen. Major Friedrich Walter Bernhard Kruger was placed at the head of the project, intended to ruin Britain's wartime economy.

Nine million forged notes with a total face value of £140 million—that is the conservative estimate of the amount of forged English paper money produced by the Germans in the 1939-45 war for the ambitious, but very plausible, project of disrupting the entire British economy.

Sachsenhausen camp was put at the disposal of 'Operation Bernhard' and some 300 forgers from different sources, many of them known criminals, were set to work. Among them was the Russian forger par excellence, Solomon Smolianoff, whose final touch perfected the plates.

The failure of the plan was in no way due to any inability of the forgers to produce notes that could fool the world —but simply that the men who made them, convicted Jewish forgers and concentration camp technicians released specially for this work, were in no hurry to complete the project. They felt, and events showed them to be right, that the moment they completed the task they would be exterminated. Major Kruger had their interests at heart for another reason. He is reputed to have told them: 'If we don't slow down I will be sent to the Russian front to fight and you will all be shot!'

The operation was revealed when a German officer surrendered himself to the Americans in Austria. With him was a lorry with 23 stout boxes containing something like £21 million worth of English notes. The captured German officer led Scotland Yard investigators to the village of Redl Zipf, where they found the machinery, but not the plates. Inquiries among the inhabitants revealed that the forgers had been sent for extermination at Ebensee.

Armed with information from the

125 The white British 'fiver' signed by Peppiatt was one of the most forged notes of the war

meticulous camp records, the Secret Service discovered that 140 of the forgers had been released. The greatest man-hunt of the war was now on. It was given as much priority as tracking down the leading Nazis who were still at large. After some 40 had been found the Allies traced the most important man, Oskar Skala, who was unobtrusively selling beer near Pilsen when the agents arrested him. A political prisoner of the Germans, Skala had been the chief book-keeper for the whole project.

It was from him that the Allies learned how the Bank of England had nearly gone bust! Heinrich Himmler had set up the organisation—Office 6-F-4—and in 1942 Major Kruger had been appointed to direct the project. Finding the printers at the Reichsbank too Prussian in their outlook, he recruited his forgers from the concentration camps which held some of the finest forgers in Europe.

At Sachsenhausen these men were put in a compound guarded by the hand-picked men of the Deathshead Brigade and instructed to forge notes. Nothing was denied them. Even normal war production was interrupted to supply the machinery the men wanted.

When the forged notes began pouring off the presses they were sent round the Gestapo representatives in Turkey, Spain, Switzerland and other neutral countries. The majority of the notes were accepted without any trouble at all. Agents coming to Britain—one was captured at Edinburgh with a suitcase stuffed full of 'fivers'—were loaded with the money. And the Germans paid off their informers with the forged money. Indeed the world-famous spy 'Cicero', who thought he was the highest-paid spy ever when he received £300,000 for secrets he took from the British ambassador's safe

at Ankara, was in fact paid with the forged money.

The forged notes fell into three groups. Grade One forged notes were put into use in neutral countries where they were used by spies. For paying collaborators, the Germans used Grade Two notes which were not quite so good but which nevertheless fooled nearly everyone except the staff of the Bank of England. Grade Three notes, good enough to fool the British public, were stored up ready to be dropped by the multi-million from aeroplanes on to the British population who, with some justification, the Germans anticipated would receive them with pleasure. Grade One notes are now known to have been paid out in Germany, gone through neutral countries to England and then back again to Germany.

But when the production rate was reaching 50,000 notes a month Kruger and the forgers began to worry. The Russian front was inside Germany and the Allies on the Western front were pushing hard. To keep all his men busy the major embarked on another ambitious programme. He started to forge American dollars as well and told his superiors that he would destroy the economy of the United States at the same time.

Soon Sachenhausen came within the fighting zone. Some of Hitler's staff wanted to close it down but Kruger, aware of the implications, argued the value of such a plant for supplying forged money and papers to senior Germans in the event of a complete collapse—which was now a certainty anyway.

As far as can be ascertained £3 million worth of these notes was used in France and the Low Countries; nearly £8 million was used in Spain, Portugal,

Switzerland and Scandinavia. £37 million escaped destruction at the end of the war when the forgers decided to store some for the future. They hid them in coffin-sized boxes in the River Enns and Lake Toplitz—but one lorry was intercepted in transit. Also some of the boxes broke open in the water and Allied servicemen went fishing with the local inhabitants. However, the Bank of England issued new £5 notes with metallic strips!

Sachsenhausen, like other camps had its own internal money. It was an ironic situation for the special guards assigned to the camp to be using internal money of 0.50 and 1 Reichsmark while millions of pounds were being produced in the same place.